Making a choice

And the coaching conversation

Ian F Farrington

The Choir Press

Copyright © 2023 Ian F Farrington

All rights reserved. No part of this publication may be reproduced or transmitted in any form or by any means, electronic or mechanical including photocopying, recording or any information storage or retrieval system, without prior permission in writing from the publishers.

The right of Ian F Farrington to be identified as the author of this work has been asserted by him in accordance with the Copyright, Designs and Patents Act 1988.

First published in the United Kingdom in 2023 by

The Choir Press

ISBN 978-1-78963-373-3

Copyright and my usage

I have made every effort to respect others' copyright in creating this book. Direct quotations and citations are all referenced. Images have been used under appropriate licences. I have sought at all times to represent the original material fairly and to meet fair use standards by only using the minimum content I needed to demonstrate how the material integrates with my approach to improving practitioner/client understanding and outcomes.

Permissions relating to any material in this work for which I hold copyright

Copyright is intended to provide legitimate protection for a person's unique idea(s), whether expressed in writing or other media. For many, however, the copyright discussion can be complex, fraught and intimidating. This can create the sense that attempts to apply copyright provisions actively want to discourage open, honest and constructive debate. In a bid to provide clarity, for my own material at least, I make the following statement.

Within the general position that all relevant rights are reserved, in relation to copyright held by me/Prodevuk® Limited:

- ☐ I permit anyone to cite/reference this work[1]
- ☐ I permit anyone to make brief quotations, reproduce 2 diagrams, or summarise my ideas in this work, provided in each case that:
    - ☐ The material is accurate
    - ☐ The use of the material fairly represents what I have said
    - ☐ Attribution to me/Prodevuk® Limited as appropriate is clear
    - ☐ This work is appropriately cited/referenced.

  For the purposes of this permission, 'brief' means 50 words or fewer per quotation, total words quoted to be fewer than 150 words. Any summarised material should be 300 words or fewer in total.

- ☐ Any substantial quotations or summarised material, or use of more than 2 diagrams requires prior written permission of the copyright holder. For the purposes of this requirement, 'substantial' means: totalling more than 150 quoted or 300 summarised words. Any request for permission will need to show as a minimum that:
    - ☐ The proposed content is accurate
    - ☐ The use of the material fairly represents what I have said
    - ☐ Attribution to me/Prodevuk® Limited as appropriate is clear
    - ☐ This work is appropriately cited/referenced.

---

[1] I'll be honest, I thought this was a clear given until I started my copyright discussions. So, the statement is included for the avoidance of doubt.

Contents

Introduction ... ix

I How did 'I' get here? ... 1

1. The grey matters ... 2
   1.1 Unexpected power ... 2
   1.2 Thought seems to be an afterthought ... 4
   1.3 Specialisation ... 6
   1.4 The emergence of patterns ... 10
   1.5 Patterning the future ... 13
   1.6 And then there's emotion ... 15
   1.7 The power of 'ish' ... 19
   1.8 A word about memory ... 22
   1.9 The grey matters ... 24
2. The brain's strange universe ... 26
   2.1 Time isn't what you will think it was ... 26
   2.2 Risk and reward ... 28
   2.3 Conscious and subconscious ... 29
   2.4 Patterns ... 30
3. Some common patterns ... 36
   3.1 Storytelling – the pattern pattern ... 36
   3.2 Causal patterns ... 38
   3.3 Framing patterns ... 40
   3.4 Authority patterns ... 43
   3.5 Overconfidence patterns ... 47
   3.6 Tied patterns ... 49
4. Beliefs, values and drivers ... 54
   4.1 Beliefs ... 54
   4.2 Values ... 57
   4.3 Drivers ... 59
   4.4 A final word on patterns ... 60

Contents

5. Errors in the machine	62
5.1 Physical effects	63
5.2 User error	64
5.3 Errors of influence	64
5.4 The truth is out there	66
5.5 The brain's strange universe – again	67
6. So, how did 'I' get here?	70
6.1 'I' as mythical entity	71
6.2 'I' as emergent property	72
6.3 Magic or complexity?	75
6.4 A need to be seen	76
6.5 A question of choice	77
6.6 How did 'I' get here?	79

II Coaching with 'I' – the coaching landscape   81

7. The coaching context	83
7.1 The inner context	84
7.2 The outer context	88
7.3 Keeping the focus on the coachee	89
7.4 Where does all that leave us?	90
8. Insights from the world of learning and development	93
8.1 Learning and learning styles	95
8.2 Conditions for effective learning	98
8.3 The coach's role supporting learning and development	101
9. The core coaching intentions: expose, explore, evolve	106
9.1 Expose, explore, evolve	106
9.2 The importance of evidence	112
9.3 Tools to expose, explore. evolve	114
10. Models for talking about the mind	116
10.1 System I, System II Thinking	118
10.2 The Chimp Paradox	120
11. Coaching focus	124
11.1 Corporate client focus	124
11.2 Coachee focus	126

III Coaching with 'I' – some of the practical implications   133

12. Contracting for coaching   135
   12.1 Stakeholder aims and authority map   139
   12.2 Coachability   141
   12.3 Commercial accountabilities   144
   12.4 Metrics   147
13. Getting the coaching work started   159
   13.1 Establishing a baseline   159
   13.2 Completing an assessment   162
   13.3 Resisting the answer   166
   13.4 Using media effectively   169
14. Common challenges   173
   14.1 Making a choice   173
   14.2 Making a choice about direction   179
   14.3 Making a choice about belonging   183
   14.4 Making a choice about unhelpful habits   189
   14.5 Making a choice about balance   195
   14.6 Making a choice   200

Conclusion   202
Afterword   205
Notes   208
Index   234

Acknowledgements

I owe a debt of gratitude to many colleagues, peers and clients over the years, who have all contributed to my developing thinking. I am especially grateful to Gilly Coubrough Crompton and Al Ritchie for their support, advice and constructive challenge as I brought this book to life. Finally, a heartfelt thanks to Miles, Adrian and Rachel at The Choir Press, for restoring faith.

Introduction

Who is this book for?

This book is intended for:

- ☐ Anyone using coaching, whether as independent or internal coaches, or as part of their leadership or management skillset.

- ☐ Customers/clients of coaching, especially the book's first two parts, which contain information that may help those readers better understand and make the most of their coaching investment. Full group or team coaching is not in scope for this volume, though the basic ideas may be used in those contexts too.

What is this book about?

The book is intended as a contribution to the coaching conversation about making a choice to take greater charge of our lives. In that context, and as an executive coach, I explore aspects of theory and practice relating to:

- ☐ **Better choice-making.** Much of our decision-making is subconscious. The central argument here is that if we become more conscious in making our key choices, we are likely to see better results for ourselves and those around us. To that end, I look at how the workings of the brain can both help and hinder our decision-making.

- ☐ **The role of coaching as we support coachees looking to *make more of their choices*.** Coaching is about working with coachees to empower them to identify and pursue solutions and strategies that best meet their needs. A better understanding of how the

Introduction

brain works should help us improve coaching performance and better serve our coachees.

Training (transfer of technical knowledge/skills) and mentoring (transfer of contextual knowledge about the sector, professional discipline or particular organisation) both have their part to play in development. For simplicity, however, I keep to a narrow coaching focus in this book.

The book's structure

The book follows a broad storyline from how the brain seems to work and what that means for some of our thoughts and behaviours, through what all that may mean for our approach to coaching; and the practical business of setting up and managing a coaching relationship. We then move on to the impact of what's going on in our heads on some of the more common choices and decisions that feature in coaching sessions. Hence, the book is in three main parts:

- □ *How did 'I' get here?* We are instinctively confident about what we mean when we say 'I' and our sense of self or personality. The picture is, however, more complex than we assume. I therefore start by trying to 'get under the hood' of how we think. So this section looks at:

    - □ The brain and its basic mechanics

    - □ What we understand of the processes of perception and thinking; and how these appear to come together to generate a sense of self, of personality and patterns of engaging with 'other' (in its simplest form, everything that's not 'I'). These all come together to create our sense of 'I'.

This section is not a comprehensive or detailed 'neuroscience 101', but it does look to capture material which is relevant to the more common challenges that coachees may face. I have attempted to reflect current thinking correctly, if in simplified form.

Introduction

- *Coaching with 'I': the coaching landscape.* This section of the book then looks at the implications of how our brains and minds work for how we (ideally coaches *and* coachees) might approach and prepare for coaching engagements. In particular, we look at the coaching context and incorporating our new insights about the brain into insights from the world of learning and development. I discuss how that then plays into the tools and techniques we might want to use – and look at models for talking about the mind with our coachees. Finally, we look at the main stakeholder focuses when it comes to coaching.

- *Coaching with 'I': some of the practical implications.* This section considers how our new understanding might shape the way we contract for coaching. We then explore getting the coaching work started, before finishing with a brief dive into some of the more common areas in which we could all benefit from trying to make more (conscious) choices.

I have included a Notes section at the back, which contains three types of comment:

- References. Specific citations are indicated in the main text and then referenced in the normal way.

- Signposts. In some of the areas I discuss, I am reflecting a common opinion or my own conclusions, based on research across many and varied authors. To keep things simple, rather than a dry bibliography, I have commented on the research I did and indicated material I found useful as starting points or travelling companions, in the hope that you find them useful too.

- Ornaments. As subjects to study/discuss, the brain and 'I' are fascinating and complex, with many, many paths and sub-paths to pursue. When reviewing my material with peers, there was a clear temptation to throw everything, including the kitchen sink, into the main text. To try to resist that urge, I have included

Introduction

some additional commentary/extended exploration of ideas/themes. They are not strictly necessary to the main text (hence 'ornaments'), but you may nonetheless find them interesting or helpful.

In pulling material and ideas together, I have followed three basic principles:

- ☐ I have quite deliberately focused on ideas that seem to help and work together. I have drawn from multiple disciplines and theoretical 'schools'. In doing that, I have not been constrained by one school's perspective or another.

- ☐ There is a vast amount of information out there about the subjects I cover. The interconnected nature of so much of what happens in our heads – and of how we engage with 'other'- makes all of it in some way relevant. To keep focused, I have tried to stick closely to the factors/coaching dialogue most relevant to making a choice.

- ☐ I can only take a snapshot of the evidence. Not only is a lot of information available, the relevant science (e.g. neuroscience, neuroeconomics, psychology) is active and dynamic. Our understanding is therefore improving by the day. Even in the time I have spent producing this book, our knowledge will have advanced.

As a result, this is not a complete examination and there will be loose ends. But, if you are encouraged to explore further, then this book will have done its job.

Why this book?

This journey started with my trying to understand, as a coach, how beliefs, values and drivers came about. In particular, I wanted to understand how sometimes these could be working against us, yet we hold onto them despite compelling evidence. In practice, this was not a straightforward journey, especially given a focus on the end-to-end story of coaching and decision-making in the business or organisational context. Why does that matter? Because of the role beliefs, values, drivers and other patterns of thought play in the choices/decisions we make.

We tend to think of ourselves as smart beings making decisions about everything, be it breakfast choices, buying houses, or major investment programmes at work. We are actively encouraged to engage in career planning and mapping our professional journey from start to finish. All this 'decision-making' encourages us in the notion of control, the notion that we are always actively steering our own path.

In reality, however, things are a bit more complex – and conscious choice features rather less often in our actions than we think. As a result, we can all too often sleepwalk, repeatedly, into situations that are uncomfortable and even self-defeating and damaging.

For sensible biological reasons, the brain tries to limit the number of conscious decisions we make. But, as a direct consequence, we may not:

- ☐ Realise we've made a decision, or
- ☐ Be making the best decision available to us.

We can, therefore, find ourselves unwittingly repeating patterns of behaviour in our personal relationships and in our work life, some of which may not serve our best interests. Worse, because we cannot see how our subconscious decisions are a large part of the problem, we do not understand why things are going off track. So we plough on, *not* making the choices that matter to us.

As coaches, we typically find ourselves working with coachees once their patterns have become unhelpful and their thoughts have become stuck. Change can be difficult because it can be hard work to change habits (ask anyone who's ever tried to give up smoking). The patterns and habits that invisibly underpin our brains and minds at work are

Introduction

interconnected in deep and complex ways, making the challenge to change all the harder. As a coach, I have certainly found myself over the years seeking ways to help coachees unpick those patterns and habits. I therefore wanted to find a more systematic way to help my coachees do that.

Some points about the language used in the book

Coaches often refer to all their customers as 'clients', but there are two distinct types: *individual coachees* and *corporate clients* (who purchase coaching services for their staff). Coachees and corporate clients have different interests and needs in relation to coaching. So, for clarity, I will use 'coachee' and 'corporate client' throughout to distinguish between the two.

I use *choice* and *decision* more or less interchangeably throughout the book. I am aware there is some active and seemingly heated debate about the difference in meaning between the two (see the Afterword). For the purposes of this book, please accept that:

- ☐ If you don't concern yourself about a difference between choice and decision, then it doesn't matter.
- ☐ If you do see a difference between the two, then read the text as meaning both.

Finally, because I see this book as part of a conversation, the style is deliberately less formal than might usually be the case.

I
How did 'I' get here?

So much of what we deal with in coaching involves exploring ways of thinking and feeling, re-setting approaches to problems and so on. All of this is realised first in the mind – and therefore through the workings of the brain. So, this section takes a brief look at how the brain seems to operate and how that plays into mind, thought and behaviour. In particular, we look at how relatively simple processes can build complex and often intractable attitudes/mindsets, some valuable, some less so.

In this part, we consider:

- ☐ The brain itself: its sheer power and basic functions; how the brain tries to save energy and resource through specialisation, using patterns and approximation; and the role of memory (chapter 1).

- ☐ The implication of the brain's workings for how we see the universe and time; and the effect that our reliance on patterns can have (chapters 2 and 3).

- ☐ The role of some special patterns (beliefs, values and drivers) (chapter 4).

- ☐ The significance of error and manipulation – and the difficulty with truth (chapter 5).

- ☐ Finally, what all this means for 'I' and, in particular, having more control over our choices (chapter 6).

1
The grey matters

As much valuable research as there has been, we are still in the early stages of really understanding our brain, never mind the trickier questions about mind and personality. To keep things manageable, we will not go into lots of biological detail – plenty of other books do that very well. So, I have focused on:

- ☐ The main things that we already know, with some sense of insights emerging from research, where this seems helpful.
- ☐ Those factors that appear most relevant to how the brain interprets the worlds of 'I' (who/what I am) and 'other'. This process of interpretation is central to how we understand – and misunderstand – our situation and opportunities. It is therefore central to the coaching dialogue that we will explore later in the book.

1.1 Unexpected power

Imagine something that could hold myriad thoughts simultaneously; that could conceive of the shape of the universe both in its vastness and at the subatomic level; that could create beauty in art and language; that could connect at a deep and sustained level with other like objects.

Now, I am fairly confident that the image that the vast majority of you conjured up did not look like the average human brain.

As an object, the brain is relatively small, averaging some 1200-1400g in weight. It is rather soft, indeed fragile, and it is not especially attractive to look at. So, on the face of it, it is not an obvious starting point for the wonder that is the human journey.

The brain – standard outer view

Image by: Pixabay openclipart

The image above is a fairly standard view of the exterior of the brain. As an object, the brain is difficult to read: the zones identified, for example, bear no obvious sign of their purpose or capability.

The brain has been extensively examined, measured and mapped inside and out over many years. We have made progress analysing and understanding brain, thought and mind. But it is still only with recent advances in technology that we are beginning to see just how the engine of thought and mind, the live brain, actually works. The research is complex and difficult, but we are, step by step, building our knowledge of how our brain does its thing.

The unprepossessing organ that is our brain is host to something approaching 100 billion neurons, capable of a hundred trillion connections. It has been calculated that the brain is capable of working at the equivalent of 1 exaflop per second (1×10^{18} 'floating point operations' per second). At the time of writing, this makes the brain's computational power greater than any known computer. The current best contender is the Japanese Fugaku supercomputer, which has been measured at c440 petaflops ($1x10^{15}$ per second). By comparison, the latest smartphones, which impress most of us on a daily basis, are rated at about 15 teraflops ($1x10^{12}$ per second). So, as much as you may love your new phone, your brain is still literally a million times more powerful!

1.2 Thought seems to be an afterthought

We are so accustomed to talking about the brain in terms of a thinking machine that we tend to take thinking as the brain's primary purpose. Actually, this does not seem to be the case. When we consider what it does, first and foremost, the brain looks like a management system for dealing with a whole range of sensory input. More pointedly, the level of sensory management needed to maintain the body may be what has driven the development of the brain (Barrett, 2020).

If thought is the child of a brain built for sensory input management, we ought to take a moment to think about what that management process may look like. Most of us were brought up with the notion that there are five senses. But the news is getting out that this is a major understatement. The current research consensus seems to be that there are nine senses:

- ☐ Sight
- ☐ Smell
- ☐ Taste
- ☐ Touch
- ☐ Hearing
- ☐ Heat
- ☐ Balance
- ☐ Pain
- ☐ Position

Beyond these nine, there is a growing body of research and evidence which points to 15, 21, 33 or even as many as 55 senses. Whatever the number, all our senses use sensors around our body that detect relevant stimuli (from within and outside the body) and send data to the brain for processing. The processing of each bit of data is driven by a range of neurotransmitters, chemical flows that drive neuron activity.

You will almost certainly have heard of dopamine and serotonin, the poster boys of the neurotransmitter world. In fact, there are several neurotransmitters that work either alone or in combination with others in order to help the brain make sense of what is going on. This process – this constant management of data, the constant ebb and flow of neurotransmitters – is going on all of the time. The result is a complex, dynamic and endlessly shifting chemical cocktail within the brain.

One of the common myths about the brain is that we are only ever using a small percentage of it. But it's easy to see that the:

- ☐ Continuous processing of all that sensory data
- ☐ Making sense of that input
- ☐ Sifting through what matters and what does not and then deciding on an appropriate response

actually starts to add up to an awful lot of brain activity.

If we do stop to think about how our brain works, we are likely to assume that the brain is somehow capturing a 'true' view of what is out in the world. It is not. The brain is only ever dealing with biochemical signals which it then has to interpret. This is a bit like only ever communicating in Morse code: we can generate meaning through the dots and dashes, but never directly experience the language, never mind the universe, that sits behind the code.

So, when I 'see' a book, the experience is representative rather than direct. My senses provide an array of data *about* this thing called a book, which I connect to memories of similar data, such as size, weight, smell, 'colour' (i.e. signals in the visible light spectrum) that help us construct *an idea* of a book. But, still, this is never a direct appreciation of the thing itself.

This sort of thinking will jar against our instinctive sense that we know what a book is. The idea that experience is indirect might feel new and challenging. However, humans have been thinking about the problem for some time. About 2,500 years ago, the philosopher Plato gave us an image of prisoners in a cave who were only ever able to see the shadows of 'other'.

Perhaps inevitably, the prisoners come to view the shadows (a representation) as reality. This belief becomes so deeply rooted that even if one prisoner escapes, sees the 'true' world and returns to tell his former cave-mates, they will (potentially with violence) reject his claims.

The relationship between our brain and 'other' is not so simple, then. If constructing the universe of 'other' inside the mind of 'I' is part of the brain's job, perhaps we should not be so surprised about how powerful the brain needs to be.

All of that brain power comes at a cost:

- ☐ It takes time to develop a human brain – typically around 25 years before it stabilises, though it never quite stops evolving.
- ☐ It is difficult to maintain brain capability – use or lose it is the key here and there is the constant threat of damage from accident or disease, which increases with age.
- ☐ Running a brain takes a lot of calories, not just enough food, but the right food to keep it going effectively.
- ☐ Trying to focus on everything all the time would be exhausting and in the end overwhelming.

Not surprisingly, the brain looks for ways to be more efficient in order to make life easier. It turns to specialisation, patterns and approximation.

1.3 Specialisation

Work takes energy. More work means using up more time, resources and energy. So, when there is a lot of work to do and much of it is similar or just plain repetitive, it makes sense to try to be more efficient. In the workplace, this led to ideas such as ergonomics, with people and teams taking on more specialised roles and repeatable actions within a larger process. By reducing complex behaviour to simple actions, each action can be performed more quickly and with less effort. In principle, if we do this for every action, the *whole* behaviour happens faster and with less effort. Not surprisingly, the brain tries to do something similar for itself.

At the higher level, the brain seems to make a broad distinction between its left and right-hand sides, allocating at least some of its processes to one side or the other. Rather curiously in this set up, the left-hand side of the brain seems to hold sway over the right-hand side of the body and vice versa.

At the same time as specialisation can improve efficiency, it raises the question of risk. What happens if, say, a part of the brain that has adapted to specialised activity becomes damaged somehow?

Current evidence suggests that at least some areas of the brain have a relatively fixed purpose/relationship – e.g. data from each of our different sets of sensors largely seem to arrive at their own dedicated areas of the brain. How much might we lose, then, if those parts of the brain were damaged somehow? Actually, the evidence is clear that in many cases the brain can adapt very successfully and often achieve performance similar to what it once had. This ability of the brain to change and adapt (neuroplasticity) is further proof of just how amazing the brain really is.

Early attempts to provide a more specific mapping of brain activity led to phrenology – a fun parlour game 'reading' the shape of a head, but long left behind by advances in psychology, medicine and neuroscience. For quite some time, one mapping has appeared to provide a stable and useful reference point: the so-called Brodmann map. Evidence from more recent neuroscientific research is pointing to a richer, more complex reality, but this map is a good enough starting point for our purposes.

Let us take a brief look at where we seem to be. The diagrams and table below provide an outline of the basic areas of the brain, the Brodmann map areas and, combined with more recent neuroscientific thinking, the emerging links between those areas and different types of brain activity.

The basic idea is that certain activities activate (and so are in some sense performed by) different parts of the brain. Advances in brain imaging technology have identified a richer pattern of activation than was previously understood.

The Brain – Brodmann area mapping

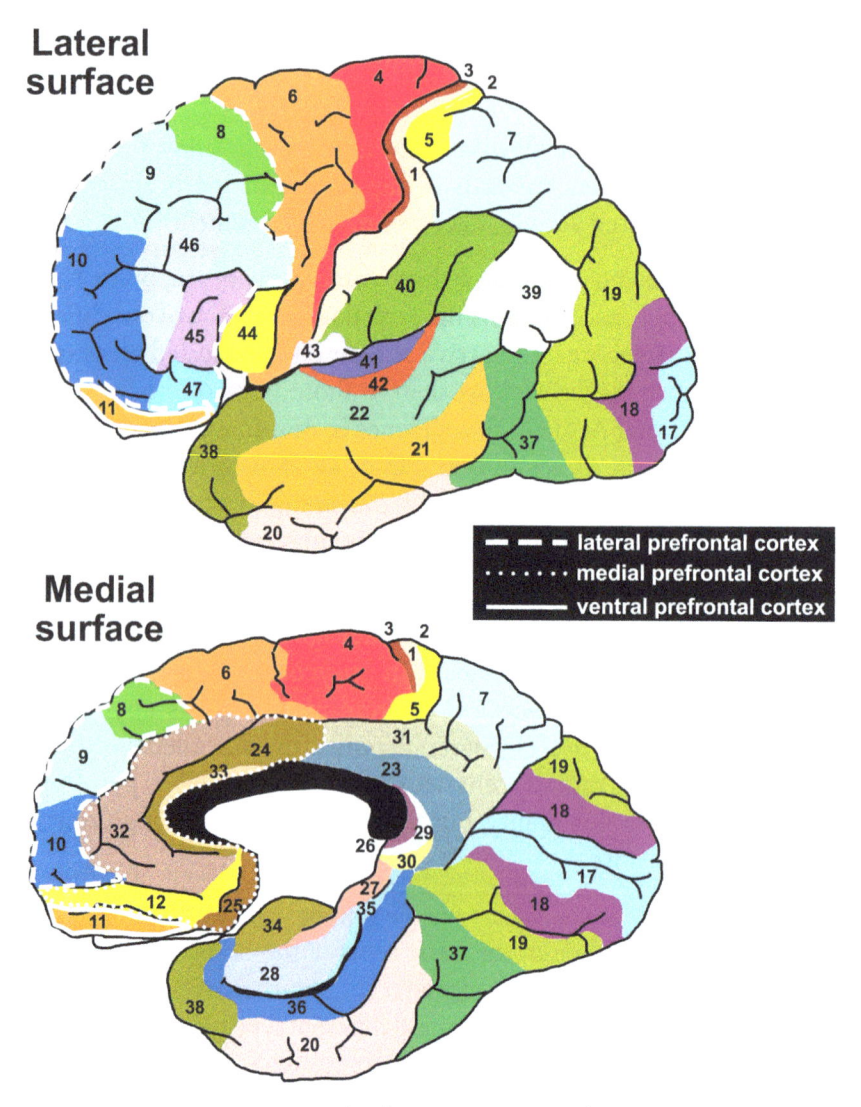

Lateral surface

Medial surface

- - - lateral prefrontal cortex
······ medial prefrontal cortex
—— ventral prefrontal cortex

Brodmann areas (image by: vishy on wiki commons)

Mapping of Brodmann areas to functional activity

Function		Brodmann area	Function	Brodmann area
Vision			Taste	43
	Primary	17	Smell	27 + olfactory bulb
	Secondary	18, 19, 20, 21, 28, 37		
Audition			Speech	22, 44, 45
	Primary	41	Cognition	
	Secondary	22, 42		
Body sensation			Perception	23, 24, 26, 29, 30, 31, 32, 33, 40
	Primary	1, 2, 3	Recognition	32, 33, 37
	Secondary	5, 7		
	Tertiary	2, 22, 37, 39, 40	Memory	23, 29, 30, 31, 32, 33, 34, 35, 36, 46
Motor				
	Primary	46	Language	39, 40
	Secondary	86	Decision making	24, 25, 38, 46
	Tertiary	9, 10, 11, 45, 46, 47		
	Eye movement	8	Self-control	23, 24, 25, 31, 32, 33
	Spatial	39, 49	Error detection	24, 32, 33
			Emotion	38

The table reflects results from both Brodmann mapping (wiki version) and subsequent neuroscientific research.

A couple of things are worth drawing out from this mapping/research results. First, it seems that very few processes activate just one area of the brain. Second, most of the underlying experiments tend to focus on specific actions (in order to provide a clear scientific baseline for analysis). Yet if we take the simple case of recognising a friend in the street, that requires:

- ☐ Sifting through the range of data provided by the sensors
- ☐ Identifying a pattern that requires analysis (i.e. that shape that looks like your friend)
- ☐ Conducting the analysis, which includes consulting the memory
- ☐ Reaching the conclusion that this is our friend
- ☐ Determining an appropriate action
- ☐ Instructing the body to complete that action.

So numerous brain areas need to activate in order to complete a relatively simple task.

Throughout this busy process of recognition, of course, the body is still sensing and processing like mad (noises, smells, the approaching child buggy, avoiding that thing on the pavement that we had rather not seen, not forgetting why we have come to the market in the first place …). Lots of areas in the brain are therefore working both on the task you are focused on (which in this case presents as the inner question: who is that?) as well as all the other activity that ensures you keep you safe. Without a degree of specialisation, the brain would struggle to cope with all this input and serve its main functions. By allocating tasks to separate areas, the brain can make the effort at least a bit more manageable.

1.4 The emergence of patterns

A further way to improve efficiency and save fuel is to create patterns for those things that happen on a regular basis. The brain does this too – a lot. The brain makes extensive use of short-cuts to help it think quickly and efficiently (the so-called *heuristic* approach). As we shall see, patterns form a large part of the brain's *heuristic toolbox*.

In our first encounter with 'other', our reaction is likely to have the following basic features:

- ☐ Experience – we interact with 'other' in whatever way it presents. The experience generates sensory data.

- ☐ Cognition – we process the sensory data to create an

- ☐ Assessment – working out the who, what, how of the experience, whether it is safe or threatening, pleasurable or painful etc. to reach an overall

- ☐ Judgement on this experience, which may produce a response (we smile, we run away etc.).

So far, so good. But that one mundane instance is not a pattern. How do we move from a single response to an enduring disposition – a pattern? It seems likely that we crystallise experiences and thoughts into patterns through:

- ☐ An overwhelming event. This is an experience so powerful that it indelibly shapes our thinking. We're most familiar with negative experiences – such as near-death experiences – not least because they have been the focus of a lot of research for practical public health reasons. But what about the potential for more 'positive' experiences, e.g. religious conversion? Saul's experience on the road to Damascus would be an obvious example. The point is that positive and negative events can both have an overwhelming impact.

- ☐ A process of iteration that creates patterns of experience which then fix as ideas/knowledge/belief. Beyond the very first experience, the brain is always looking to assess its current experience both in the light of the basic signals it's receiving and of past experience. Once an experience – or something similar to it – begins to be repeated, the brain recognises the similarity and starts to map its perception of that past experience to the current one. A pattern begins to emerge.

For most of us, overwhelming events are likely to be few and far between. Iteration is therefore likely to be the dominant route to building patterns of thought.

Note here that we have introduced memory to the process. I will talk a little more about memory later, but the key point is that the ability to store *and* recall information is absolutely critical to the brain's ability to compare experiences and construct an appropriate response. Without memory, we would be stuck in and be overwhelmed by the present. Consider the distress caused by amnesia, whether retrograde (loss of memories, typical in Alzheimer's) or anterograde (inability to form new memories). Memory, which we tend to think of as a key to the past, in effect plays a key role in coping with the present and our sense of existing in time.

For most of us, our earliest memories – and earliest patterns – will relate to experiences such as warmth, safety, fear, belonging, reward or punishment. These are natural reactions as we come to terms with our existence in the context of family and the larger world. Unfortunately for some, there will be traumatic experiences and memories too. These early memories – and the patterns they generate – tend to crystallise when we are young. This matters because it means the patterns are hard-set before we:

- ☐ Really have control over language, or
- ☐ Have developed an ability to describe and analyse what has happened clearly.

If these first patterns are so deep-rooted and beyond articulation, it's no surprise then that they can prove so powerful and resistant to evolution/adaptation in our adult years.

1.5 Patterning the future

We begin with a series of similar experiences. The brain starts to notice similarities between those experiences. It also starts to notice that its mapping or anticipation of them proves to be a good enough representation for its needs. At this point, the brain will start to treat the emerging pattern as an effective template for appraising any repeat or similar experience. The value of this use of a pattern is twofold:

- ☐ In the face of a new experience, we can much more quickly determine an appropriate response. The sense of threat from an unexpected experience will be reduced. Even if the right thing to do is to run away, we will feel more in control of understanding why and of carrying out the right action.

- ☐ In anticipation of the experience, we can plan our (re)action, so we can: deal more calmly with the unpleasant experience at the dentist's; have an umbrella to hand because it has rained every other public holiday this year; or have answers ready to the customer's probable follow up questions at the sales meeting.

A pattern is deemed successful insofar as it generates an apparently effective and predictable response. The more a pattern 'delivers', the more trusted it becomes.

Successful patterns save calculating time and energy. They provide a sense of context and clarity for what is happening now; and can help prepare for and de-risk the future. This makes patterns really powerful and attractive. No surprise, then, that the brain is an eager pattern maker.

1.5.1. My lucky ...

A sufficiently well-embedded pattern can take on extra powers – it may become knowledge or a belief. Indeed, we can move with surprising ease through a cognitive cycle producing judgements evolving as:

- ☐ We won the game yesterday ...
- ☐ We have won 4/5 games – I wore my blue t-shirt in the 4 winning games ...
- ☐ We win whenever I wear my blue t-shirt ...
- ☐ If I wear my lucky blue t-shirt, we will win.

Now we may smile at this, but most of us have had a 'lucky blue t-shirt' at some point, even if we claimed to be wearing it ironically! But it shows that beliefs, those powerful influencers on how we interpret the world of 'other', can be founded on pretty shaky ground. Clearly, there may be an element of value in that the shirt may evoke positive thinking which then encourages positive performance, but I think we can be at least 99% sure that crediting the shirt for a win goes too far.

The relationship between the 'lucky blue t-shirt' and success is one of correlation, not cause. But if the correlation is sufficiently consistent, the brain will deem the pattern causal and successful anyway.

Through iteration and our memory, we build up a catalogue of experiences and beliefs/assumptions. Each has been shaped by how we have responded to the outer world, but also in turn influences how we approach the outer world. Thus, in any given event, our beliefs and experience are intimately linked with our thoughts, feelings and action. We can summarise this in the diagram on page 15.

The grey matters

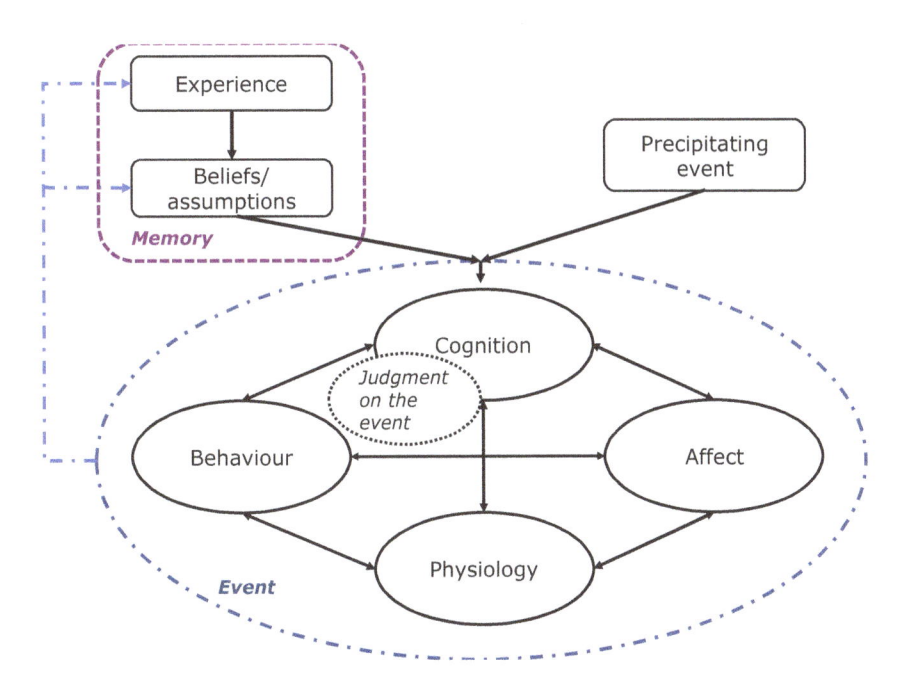

Adapted from Westbrook et al (2011)

This diagram is adapted from techniques used in Cognitive Behavioural Therapy (CBT) and Neuro-Linguistic Programming (NLP). The techniques are intended to help CBT/NLP clients break down unhelpful cycles of belief-action and then create new, more helpful thinking. They have a fairly impressive success rate – which is why the CBT versions are recommended health care treatments.

1.6 And then there's emotion

Beyond this basic cycle, it is also clear that the process contains an emotional component, whether that be instinctive (a simple reaction to pleasure, pain, fear etc.) or a slower time assessment of what has happened. The key point is that an emotional value is attached to every experience and its memory. Further, that emotional value is recalled as part of the memory and so forms part of any emerging thinking pattern. Given its prevalence, I think we represent emotion better by reflecting it *through* a cognitive model, rather than as just one sequence in a model.

The link between memory and its associated emotional value may also be what facilitates the way in which memory and emotion evoke each other. When we are in a particular emotional state, certain memories may come back into focus. If, for example, we are grieving for a current loss, we tend to recall other similar losses. Equally, when we recall a memory, or a pattern, or imagine a similar experience in the future, we may find that our emotional state changes to mirror the emotion that we associate with the relevant pattern.

Most of us have had that experience of anticipating a future event. This may be a visit to the dentist or dressing down by the boss, where we project how bad it is going to be. The anxiety is often followed by relief when things turn out not to be so bad. This may simply be because one difficult experience is not as powerful as your combined memory of a number of difficult experiences. However, if that dressing down turns out to be worse than you expected, your pattern will adjust to an even more negative tone for the next time. The key point here is that any anxiety here is fed by and fuels the emotional content of our memory.

We tend to talk about emotion and rationality as exclusive features. It seems quite clear, though, that they go hand in hand within the brain's basic processing operations. We need to remember that the emotional 'balance' in the brain relates in some degree to the chemical 'balance' within the brain. In situations we find extreme, that is likely to mean a chemical *imbalance* (e.g. that rush of fight, flight or freeze chemistry in times of threat). We might reasonably expect that same chemical rush to interfere with the brain's 'business as usual'. This seems to be the case in practice.

Most of us will recognise that in the face of extreme stress we do not behave the way we normally would. In essence, the brain is trying to find a 'safe' way out of this stress. But if fight, flight or freeze are blocked as options, the sense of confusion and stress will increase. This means that our focus tends to narrow, because we have to reduce the amount of data we're dealing with in an attempt to cope. You can see the potential for a vicious cycle here.

Now, put that into a work context. How often do people find themselves in 'firefighting' behaviours, blocked from progress by their focus on fighting the fire? The fire gets worse, they become more stressed and on it goes. We can find it impossible to break from the cycle, even if we recognise that it can harm us and those around us.

If emotion is central to the cognitive process, then our working cognitive cycle may look something like the diagram below. The brain is constantly trying to process what it thinks/feels/believes (operating in 'belief space') and working to generate/react to what it decides 'I' says/does, or what it perceives 'other' as saying/doing (events in the 'behaviour space').

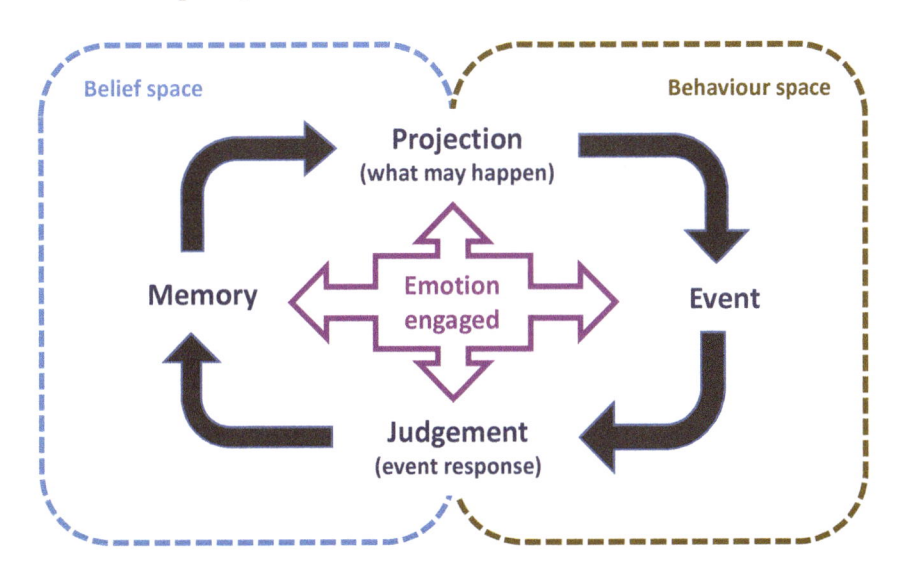

There are some important implications if we look at the cognitive cycle this way:

- ☐ Each 'event response' (which incorporates elements of cognition, affect, behaviour, physiology, beliefs etc.) is stored in some way ... typically as memory.
- ☐ Emotion is a component of the event response and what is stored.
- ☐ There is evidence of the effect of emotion on memory storage and on the positive/negative associations with a memory. Thus, emotion has a direct impact on what and how we remember – it is bound into our patterns.
- ☐ In storing (i.e. creating a memory), cognition includes an emotionally-influenced and suffused judgement on the event and event response, which then informs our memories and emerging patterns and beliefs.
- ☐ When we try to retrieve a memory, we don't remember pure objective fact, but a representation filtered through our emotional perception of what took place. This is not to deny the 'truth' of an event, merely to recognise the partiality of our recollection of it.
- ☐ When we look towards what may happen in the future, we will draw on our memory. This means that we will draw on emotionally-charged experiences and beliefs, as well as our current emotional state. These we then use in framing our attitude towards what will happen.

We have looked at this from the perspective of retrieving practical/behavioural memories, but we do experience emotion directly too. So, not only are emotions in patterns, they will also have their own patterns. Such patterns may help us recognise our own emotional state – or indeed the emotional states of others. We then adopt what we have stored as 'appropriate' behaviours/responses.

Of course, this then opens up the potential for emotion to act as a route to addressing unhelpful patterns and beliefs. Indeed, there are techniques involving disassociation, substitution and modification that seem to achieve just that. We will talk a little bit more about those later.

The intensity of the emotion associated with an experience, appears to be a clear factor in the impact of that experience (and the resulting judgement we make about it). This may go some way towards explaining why teenage and 'first' experiences form such an enduring part of our mindset (and why marketers and extremists are so keen to target the young!). The chemical cocktail in our brain seems to reach its volatile peak during our teenage years, so emotional associations with experiences are likely to be more intense in that period.

Similarly, first experiences are, by definition, a surprise and however much we may have expected and 'prepared' ourselves for a first (surprise), we have not yet lived it, so the brain has not understood the experience through its physical/chemical processes. This first memory, then, has a novelty and uniqueness which no subsequent similar experience can ever match.

There is a lot of detail to take in here. For now, the key point to remember is that the brain is engaged in a constant cognitive cycle as it does its best to make sense of 'other'/the outer world. Out of that process, the brain builds patterns of (emotional) thought to save time and energy. The patterns are generally valuable to us, but there are clearly risks too.

1.7 The power of 'ish'

The brain's 'heuristic toolbox' has another trick in it to make the brain's life easier: approximation. In principle, the brain can consciously process all incoming sensory data all of the time, even when attempting to focus on a particular issue. It is easy to see, though, how exhausting such an approach would be. Naturally, then, the brain will look to lighten the load. To achieve that, it will often find that taking an approximation serves its needs.

How did 'I' get here?

So, let's take a simple example of what approximation means in practice. Imagine the scene on a summer's day where you are outside doing something you like (taking a walk, picnicking with friends etc.). Picnicking is of course a particularly good outside activity.

Image by: Calvin Shelwel on Unsplash

Okay, have that thought in your head?

Let's assume you did indeed think about a picnic(!). You will probably have given a fair degree of thought to any individual(s) you were with and to what you were all doing at the time. The epicures among you may have paid some attention to the food and drink available, while the fashionistas among you may have thought about style specifics. But, on balance, most of you are likely to have thought rather less about what people were wearing, or the details of the space you were in, or even less the clouds above (unless your memory was specifically about a downpour!). In your imagination, you almost certainly did not spend time constructing a detailed image of the sky. Rather, your brain is more likely to have selected (recreated) a stock image of 'summer's day sky' that was good enough to serve your purpose.

This practice of approximation, of seeking enough data to meet your needs and then filling in the blanks with (usually background) things you already 'know' is an absolutely core brain habit. By mixing and matching focused attention with filling the blanks, the brain saves itself a lot of time and energy. When we are doing something habitual – e.g. the day job, the weekly shop – the brain has a fairly good idea what to expect. It can of course spin around like an eager puppy, treating every work day like a first experience. Or, it can focus on what it knows needs to be done and assume other stuff will be the same as yesterday. As long as the short-cut delivers results that are close enough to what is expected, the brain 'wins'.

We also recognise that no two experiences are exactly the same, so we have a degree of in-built tolerance for variation. As a consequence, approximation is an effective tool, so the brain uses it a lot – why wouldn't it? The risk, of course, lies in the selection of what to see and what to store.

1.8 A word about memory

I promised I would say a bit more about memory. Recall the cognitive cycle diagram:

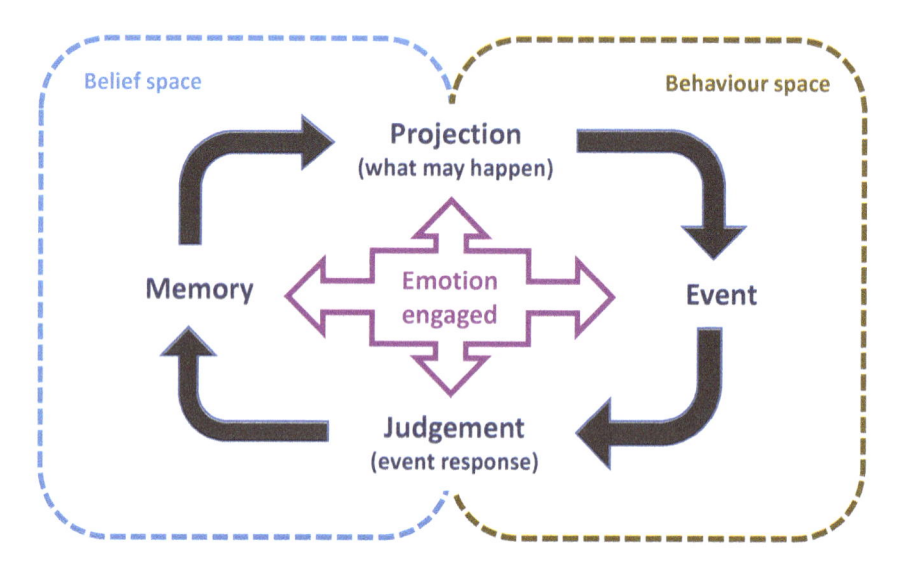

[Diagram: Cognitive cycle showing Belief space (containing Memory and Projection) and Behaviour space (containing Event and Judgement), with Emotion engaged at the centre. Projection (what may happen) → Event → Judgement (event response) → Memory → Projection.]

As we saw earlier, memory is a critical factor in the process. It follows, then, that we need our memory to be on top form to make the best of the way our brains work. Obviously, illness and damage can get in the way of that, but how memory seems to work does not entirely help either.

To begin with, a memory is a complex thing. Nor is it at all certain that memory is 'a thing'. There is continuing debate about what constitutes 'a' memory. But there is considerable evidence, especially from neuroscientific research, that points to memory as:

- A 'distributed property' (Nyberg and Cabeza, 2000). 'A' memory does not sit in one tidy corner of the brain. Instead, what is stored is held in multiple sites.
- Dependent on 'a number of associated functions' (Markowitsch, 2000). Recall the brain map of Brodmann areas

we showed earlier. Memory appears to activate many parts of the brain: 10 relevant zones have been identified so far and research continues.

The implicit consequence is that recall requires reactivating at least those parts of the brain originally involved in creating the memory and then reconstructing a memory from the different 'storage' points across the brain. This means that both 'a memory' and the memory recall process appear to be composite. The brain deconstructs and reassembles the relevant features of 'a' memory when needed. As we all know, in practice, artefacts/processes with more parts (like the memory) tend to be more vulnerable to things going wrong.

What's more, there can be some unhelpful distortions. Memory is malleable and distortion can be forward and backward in time. In other words, we can change:

- ☐ The nature of how a memory is stored
- ☐ A stored memory itself
- ☐ How that memory plays into our projection/ expectation.

We have also seen the importance of emotion in shaping a memory. This suggests that we might be able to change a memory by changing the emotions associated with it.

If the memory process can be flawed, then the stored/recalled version of an experience/belief may be flawed too (to the extent that it is simply inaccurate or even unhelpfully distorted). Moreover, the idea that memory storage and recall are complex processes, suggests that they might also be malleable or occasionally flawed.

Memory is key to shaping thought, mindset, knowledge and belief. So, if our memories may be flawed, we must recognise the potential fallibility of those thoughts and beliefs. We must recognise the potential in each of us to recall or even believe in error.

1.9 The grey matters

In this section, we have skimmed the surface of how the brain seems to work and taken a slightly deeper look into one of its core processes (memory). On the one hand, the sheer power, flexibility and adaptability of that grey mass should leave us a little awestruck – what the brain can do is a genuine marvel. But even a gentle peek under the surface shows that perhaps things are not quite as straightforward as we would like to assume.

We started out with the idea that the brain's primary focus maybe about sensory data management, rather than thinking (1.2). But that process becomes infinitely easier with memory (to recall what the data should look like) and with patterns to help manage the body in response. Already, this means that the brain is working cognitively. Start using patterns to project (a need for) action and the components for the cognitive cycle are in place. Moreover, these shortcuts create space for more complex processing – thoughts – that can yield better results (biochemical rewards) for the body and the brain. Thought may have been secondary, but it turns out to be well worth the candle – if the brain is smart about how it manages the data.

In its attempt to cope with all of whatever is out there, the brain (necessarily) takes a few shortcuts, which can produce some interesting outcomes.

Next stop – a bit more about the strange universe the brain creates.

Key takeaways

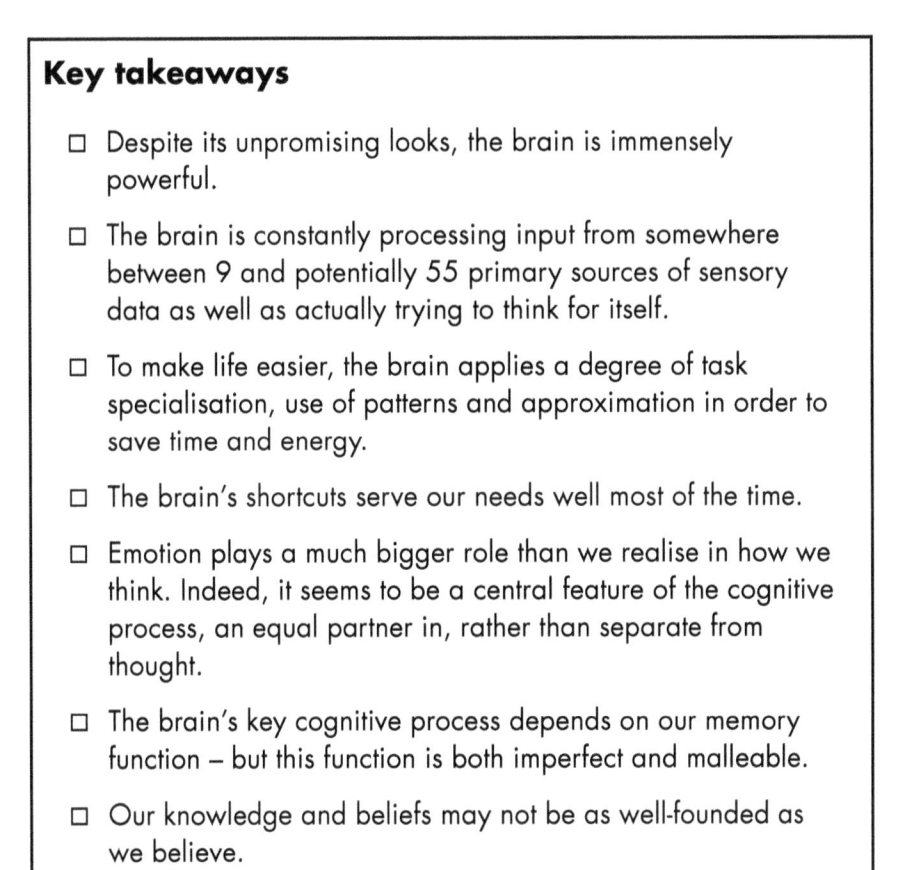

- ☐ Despite its unpromising looks, the brain is immensely powerful.
- ☐ The brain is constantly processing input from somewhere between 9 and potentially 55 primary sources of sensory data as well as actually trying to think for itself.
- ☐ To make life easier, the brain applies a degree of task specialisation, use of patterns and approximation in order to save time and energy.
- ☐ The brain's shortcuts serve our needs well most of the time.
- ☐ Emotion plays a much bigger role than we realise in how we think. Indeed, it seems to be a central feature of the cognitive process, an equal partner in, rather than separate from thought.
- ☐ The brain's key cognitive process depends on our memory function – but this function is both imperfect and malleable.
- ☐ Our knowledge and beliefs may not be as well-founded as we believe.

2
The brain's strange universe

Our brain sits at a remove from the universe of 'other', which it can only experience by interpreting the constant flow of millions of bits of sensory data. It is therefore constantly constructing a sense of what 'other' is. This process also means that the balance of neuro-chemical activity in the brain is in constant flux. All this endless activity is difficult and energy-consuming, so the brain applies a number of tricks to make its task easier. Over time, these tricks begin to have their own effect on the brain in respect to both our sense of what is out there and our sense of self.

In this section, we start to look at some of the curious results of the brain's workings and will begin with thoughts about time, risk and conscious action.

2.1 Time isn't what you will think it was

At first thought, most of us will instinctively feel we have a sense of how time works and of past, present and future. Those who have studied languages will have wrestled – and periodically lost battles – with the pluperfect and future perfect too, for example. Objectively, the concept of a timeline makes sense, even if we sometimes have to work at getting the sequence right.

The way the brain and our sense of self work means that a sense of place in time doesn't quite operate in the way we expect. For a start, our sense of self, our 'I', finds it difficult (impossible, really, but I'm trying to break it to you gently) to be simultaneously in the moment and aware. So, when we talk about 'now', that observation is an observation about a past situation. However quickly we try to force ourselves into awareness, we are already reflecting – looking back in time.

Further, if a current experience prompts our brain to apply a pattern, we are actively filtering our examination of 'now' through the past. This leads to an experience common in coaching. Most of us who are coaches will be familiar with the fact that the past is often unhelpfully present in the 'now' for our coachees. The past may surface as a problematic value, belief, or knowledge (a past judgement) shaping a coachee's thoughts and actions.

The paradox goes a step further. Our sense of the future is a form of projection from our now ('an idea in the now', Grosz, 2013). But that means that, in some sense, our sense of future is a form of our past.

When we act consciously, we can understand and work with timelines effectively, but this is not the brain's default approach. The brain is rather more ambiguous in its treatment of *was, is* and *may be*.

While this might feel like something of a rarefied philosophical debate, at some point, the consequences are tangible for us all. This brain quirk about time can have a direct impact on how any of us engage with and are treated by the world of 'other'. In particular, it can get in the way of our recognising what is actually happening.

Most of us will have learned at least one hard lesson about a past experience undermining our present. Much of this may well be trivial – the differences between acceptable behaviour in the family home and when we grow up and go to work, for example. We generally remember the bigger 'lessons', such as fears (snakes, spiders, clowns, take your pick) and how they came about. But we tend to be less conscious of the moments we learned 'I can't…'. As a result, when we find ourselves saying 'no' to something now or a future opportunity, we may not be conscious of past experience (crystallised as 'I can't') shaping our today and tomorrow. Part of a coach's role may be to help their coachee work out the timeline and evolution of unhelpful thoughts in order to make progress.

Perhaps inevitably, childhood seems to be a bottomless source of examples for many of us. These childhood (limiting) beliefs tend to be well entrenched. As a consequence, dismantling such beliefs can be a major challenge and demand sustained effort over time.

2.2 Risk and reward

As a matter of fact, we are quite good at modelling risk/chance. Essentially, we can apply probabilistic processes to a suitable range of relevant factors. We can even adjust for weighting/bias in the behaviour and interaction of factors. We can also adjust and evolve our calculations over time, becoming more accurate along the way. As a result, we can create some fairly stable and effective models of risk.

So far, so good. However, as a matter of practice, most of us can quickly get into a muddle when it comes to understanding and judging risk. It doesn't matter how clear the guidance from a relevant model is, we can find ourselves distracted because we:

- ☐ 'Know' that unexpected and unlikely outcomes are possible.
- ☐ Judge by emotion as much as evidence. So, the decision may come down to whether we feel lucky or not right now.
- ☐ Build a belief over time about whether we are lucky. This can be periodic (so we think of ourselves in a good or bad patch) or enduring.
- ☐ Are strongly influenced by our perception of risk and return/reward. Big returns can outweigh smaller ones, regardless of the chances of failure/success. We should note here that although money is an obvious incentive, it is certainly not the only one. In many cases, it may not even be in our 'top three'. The prospect of psychological reward (recognition, success, status etc.) can be powerfully motivating and can influence what we are willing to do to achieve it.

Sometimes, of course, we just fail to understand the risk. This can manifest as optimism bias, loss aversion, or 'it's my turn' thinking.

A common mistake with probability is assuming that every option comes up within a reasonable time frame. Let's consider the Euromillions lottery. Broadly, the chances of winning the jackpot are about 1/140,000,000 – but even when the lottery has been drawn 140 million times, that does *not* mean your numbers will come up. No draw directly affects another, so, for every draw, the chances of a specific set of numbers coming up remain the same. Your odds of winning are still 1/140,000,000.

We have seen that a number of factors, alone or in combination, can distort our understanding of risk/chance. As a result, for the most part, very few of us take a cool, calm, objective view of the risks/chances before us. We seem to develop a 'risk appetite' pattern of thinking, which then acts as an additional filter in our judgement process.

2.3 Conscious and subconscious

The *conscious* 'I' finds it very difficult to think and articulate about its own *subconscious*. As a result, our 'I' tends to think of material (thoughts, beliefs etc.) in the conscious space as 'complete'. By this I mean that when the conscious 'I' does step into a decision, it is likely to treat the rationale it can see as the whole story. When we decide not to go after a job because it is something we 'can't' do, we trust that 'can't' is a well-founded truth about ourselves.

The fact is, the conscious is only the tip of the iceberg when it comes to the mind. The subconscious occupies the great majority of the working space and it is generally blocked to us. As with most things the brain does, the origins of this divide lie in a good intent, but the result may not serve us well. Since we cannot see what is happening, our subconscious may be hurting us without our realising it. For decisions that matter, it seems useful to be able to bring more of what lies in our subconscious into the light of day.

This then raises a question: when the conscious 'I' has a reason for a decision, how do we know whether that is a calculated reason or the brain taking a handy short-cut?

How did 'I' get here?

Well, we need to test the logic, evidence and argument beneath the decision. If the foundations quickly wobble or evaporate, that is a pretty good hint that a short-cut is in play. That's a pretty good hint that we need to re-think.

2.4 Patterns

We have seen that, for good reasons, the brain likes patterns. As a result, it builds many patterns over its lifetime. Patterns try to make things simpler and quicker to understand (at least well enough for the brain's purposes), so tend to be helpful. Broadly, we might think about patterns working both:

- ☐ Passively: in that while the patterns are there they are usually evoked as a reaction to something;
- ☐ Actively: in that they shape our decisions and actions.

In terms of our cognitive cycle we use patterns *actively* in projection and *passively* in judgement:

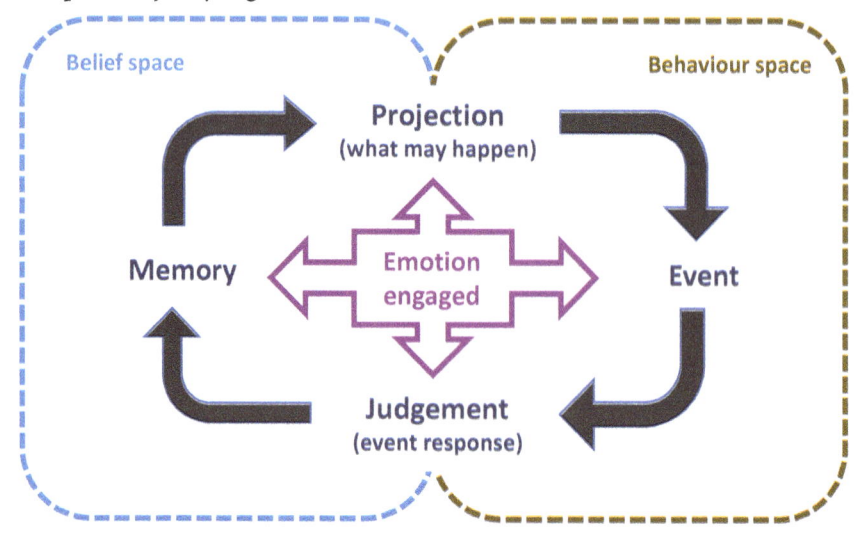

```
        Belief space                    Behaviour space
                     Projection
                   (what may happen)
                         ↕
         Memory    ⇄  Emotion  ⇄   Event
                     engaged
                         ↕
                     Judgement
                   (event response)
```

Note: this use is distinct from whether a pattern is being applied consciously or subconsciously.

30

We may therefore be:

- ☐ Consciously and actively running through our 'sales meeting' pattern ahead of a meeting.
- ☐ Subconsciously and actively worrying about getting there in time because of the train service.
- ☐ Consciously and passively assessing how well this meeting is going compared with recent successful meetings.
- ☐ Subconsciously and passively becoming a little stressed because we have a pattern that considers sitting with our back to the door as risky.

I have pared down this example for simplicity and clarity but, obviously, when consciously, actively preparing for our meeting, we may be affected by:

- ☐ Conscious and subconscious reactions to what is happening to us in the moment – how busy the train is and our tolerance for crowds.
- ☐ The carriage temperature and noise levels.
- ☐ Whether we have eaten beforehand, are eating on the train, or decided to leave it until later.
- ☐ Processing some of the events from earlier in the day (the wake-up alarm, hot water for a shower etc.).

You can readily imagine other factors that might feature for you in each of the four circumstances above. It is easy to see from this simple example, therefore, how one event can spawn myriad thoughts, each evoking one or more patterns that shape our understanding and actions. Importantly, a substantial part of that activity happens subconsciously. This means there's a good chance that our perception of the meeting, how we behave at it and what we take from it have all been shaped in large part by our own subconscious thoughts (and therefore without our being aware of it).

How did 'I' get here?

The main theme threading through this book is that the 'fun' starts when we begin subconsciously applying patterns (actively or passively) in our engagement with 'other'. Despite wanting to help, the subconscious can make mistakes. In particular, the trouble can ramp up when we (our subconscious) start to turn our patterns against our best interests. Trouble can come from external sources too. Since the brain and its workings are malleable, we can have our patterns turned against us.

2.4.1 The wrong pattern

Patterns are seductive things. The more they seem to work, the more likely we are to use them. The brain will tend to apply a 'good' pattern more confidently, more quickly.

Initially, the brain might look for half a dozen or so points of similarity. Over time, it may begin to apply a pattern after only one or two familiar points have been identified. Now, most people have been in a conversation where one person (and at some point in time, that meant us) jumped in too quickly, missed the point and either caused everyone to steer the conversation back or caused a misunderstanding, or even a full-blooded argument.

In the same way, the brain, with the best of intentions, can leap to a pattern that is not appropriate for the current circumstances – with unwelcome consequences. This may be, for example, because the pattern is:

- ☐ A bad fit (e.g. a defensive pattern built in response to unfair criticism may not help when this time we were in the wrong).
- ☐ No longer relevant (e.g. bringing a child-like behaviour into an adult context) nor meets our needs.

2.4.2 Patterns turned against us

Patterns, by their nature, are also more common and predictable than we realise. At some point in our lives, we have all experienced guilt, loneliness, joy etc. Unique as we may be as individuals, common experiences tend to provoke similar responses – and so tend to create similar patterns. If we are using similar patterns, we may take similar actions. Indeed, there are whole industries built on the idea that we can reasonably predict the responses of sufficiently large numbers of people – and that we can use that insight to shape how many of those people act.

In the commercial world, pattern exploitation often manifests as sales and marketing, with words, images and actions marshalled to guide our thinking and action. This may be as language and images used to activate our patterns around status, desire, need. But it may also include the use of:

- ☐ Light
- ☐ Scents (creating a positive, hungry atmosphere in store)
- ☐ Scale (e.g. the use of ¾ size furniture in a home for sale, to make a room look large enough to be useful)
- ☐ Movement (forcing us to follow a particular route, exploiting how our eyes tend to track an image)
- ☐ Or, indeed, some combination of these.

There is a reason we often feel we bought more than we wanted or something we didn't really want in the first place.

In the political world, pattern exploitation may manifest as spin, propaganda, division. These techniques play to our need for belonging (the 'us and them' theme is core to political diatribe); and our habit of approximation (insinuate and lead them to a desired if not well-founded conclusion).

In fairness, this can of course be a positive force: nudge techniques have demonstrably improved a number of public welfare outcomes in several countries.

In both positive and negative cases, the impression that others are speaking 'my language'/speaking 'to me' is a powerful act of recognition, of implied belonging.

The worlds of marketing and politics have developed a keen understanding of the importance of emotion in establishing attachment and reducing examination of what's really being said. As we saw earlier, emotional engagement is particularly important when we are younger. The resulting combination of emotion and activation of multiple senses can all have a powerful impact on a target audience. It's not for nothing that political youth rallies tend to be such spectacles.

2.4.3 The curious impact of 'Don't!'

One particular predictable pattern we have in common relates to the phrase 'don't'. In the majority of cases, telling someone 'don't' seems to be a sure-fire way of guaranteeing that they will. As a pattern, this behaviour establishes very early on (go to any supermarket most days of the week to see the same performance played out between parent and young child). Unfortunately, the pattern often persists into adulthood. The effects are well-documented in sports coaching, in particular, the way that focusing on not doing something (e.g. missing a pass) almost guarantees it will happen. But this is a clear phenomenon in business and other teams too.

Key takeaways

- ☐ The brain uses a number of tricks to make its life easier.

- ☐ The brain's tricks serve us well a lot of the time. But things can go awry.

- ☐ We may think we have a clear idea about past, present, future. But the brain's reliance on the past muddles its processing of time.

- ☐ Similarly, our views on risk and reward tend to be more distorted than we realise.

- ☐ The conscious is only the tip of the iceberg when it comes to thinking. The vast majority of the brain's work happens at the subconscious level. As a result, we don't understand how we made many of our decisions, nor what faults there might be in those processes.

- ☐ The brain relies heavily on the use of patterns. So long as the patterns deliver outcomes broadly consistent with our expectations, the brain will accept the pattern as valid and successful.

- ☐ If we are not mindful, patterns can be misapplied; they can be faulty; and they can actively (be made to) work against our interests.

3
Some common patterns

Given how important patterns are to our brains and to how we deal with 'other', it's worth taking a look at some of the more common ones. They all seem to make regular appearances in the coaching dialogue. I have opted for six broad themes of pattern. You can read this chapter all in one go, but it may be easier to treat it as something to dip into when you want to look at types of pattern in a bit more detail.

As you do venture into the detail, you should recognise quite a few of the patterns and that you have applied them yourself at times. Keep in mind that the reason these patterns are common is because they can serve us well in so many circumstances.

3.1 Storytelling – the pattern pattern

Once upon a time . . .

This is probably our most ingrained and most important pattern – storytelling seems to be one of the oldest activities that we humans engage in. We know that one of the brain's core functions is to consume and make sense of a wide range of streams of sensory data, linking elements together to create some coherent whole – the brain is relational from the start. But the human brain seems to go further than that, adding form and sequence to sets of relations to create a story. The pattern manifests itself in so many aspects of our life: when we talk about 'life', 'love', 'career' – all is story.

Storytelling is valuable because it assists memory, it develops the imagination and our analytical capacity. The central narrative thread can both impel us forward and hold together all the elements we need to understand and to act. Storytelling also supports the sharing of knowledge and belonging. As a species, we have been telling stories as long as we can remember. They form part of the deepest roots of our communities and culture – we identify with each other in no small part because we share one or more stories.

Where storytelling can be less helpful is in imagining relationships or pathways that are simply not there, which then leads to misunderstanding and unhelpful actions. In particular, we can become fixated with a story and begin to act as though it were true. If we treat a fable as a personal blueprint, we are likely to end up in failure, anger and despair.

3.2 Causal patterns

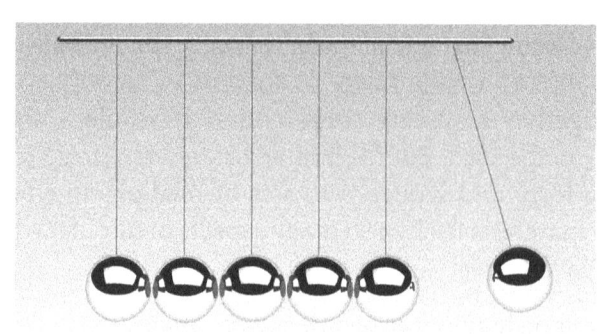

Image by: G Rezende on pixabay

This is a focus on a particular relationship between ideas and things (phenomena, more formally) – that one thing (A) gives rise to another (B). The relationship may further extend to the more forceful thought that *without* A, B would not exist. There are several patterns of this type.

3.2.1 Action causes effect

We can describe the basic variations on the theme as:

- Simple positive: A causes B – hitting the bell makes a noise.
- Simple negative: without A, B does not happen – if you don't hit the bell, there is no noise.
- Complex positive weak: A and/or C and/or D cause B. I need to get to town, it doesn't matter whether that's by train, car or bus.
- Complex positive strong: A and C and D are all required to cause B – anyone who studied history at school will have been set at least one essay asking them to 'comment on the causes of the (insert options) war'.
- Complex negative partial: if any of A, C or D is not present, then no B. If any of Jill, Jo or John fails to appear, then we won't be able to field a crew.
- Complex negative full: if all of A, C and D are absent, then no B – like simple negative, but with more failing parts!

3.2.2 Survivorship

The idea here is that we see a situation, B, and presume that the actions/conditions that precede it must have caused it. It is in effect a reverse engineering of cause. This thought underpins, for example, the rather large library of books on how to be a leader, many of which are founded on the reverse-engineered causal chain that:

- ☐ Company X is successful
- ☐ Company X is led by Mr Y
- ☐ So Mr Y's leadership of Company X caused the company's success and must therefore be the way to be successful.

3.2.3 The Placebo Effect

The central theme here is: if I believe and act as if A causes B, then B happens. We are perhaps most familiar with the concept in the health sector. The idea is easy to dismiss and clearly it can be dangerous if we start thinking we can cure cancer by dancing naked in the garden at midnight. However, the psychological power of placebo treatment is well documented, suggesting that the placebo effect can be positive in the right circumstances.

This pattern can evolve fully into magical thinking, from lucky t-shirts (we discussed earlier) to 'positive thinking', ritual and prayer. This can be powerfully motivating. However, it can cause us significant disappointment and even damage when it fails.

3.2.4 The good and the bad of causal patterns

Causal patterns can provide really useful insights into the relationships between phenomena. This can improve our understanding, performance and interaction with others.

The primary risk with causal patterns is that correlation is not the same as cause. The children's rhyme hickory dickory dock tells the brief tale of a mouse that climbs up a clock. The clock strikes the time and the mouse runs back down the clock again. Now, as a whimsy, it might please us to think that a mouse checked its wristwatch, ran up the clock, caused the hour chime to strike, then returned to its normal duties. Yet there is no evidence whatsoever of a causal relationship between the events in the rhyme. In fairness, however, you would be forgiven for a least a moment's wondering whether a clever mouse was at work here ... precisely because cause is a compelling pattern.

The potential power of causal patterns to shape our thinking is well understood in marketing circles, who regularly exploit the notion that if you buy product x your life will become somehow better: 'trust us, retail therapy creates status, happiness' etc.

The problem is, when we build our thinking and action on incorrect/false reasoning, we start to live a delusion. Delusions are not only unhelpful and unhealthy, they can become dangerous. A clock-watching mouse is innocent enough. But when the Mayans concluded that human sacrifice was necessary to appease their gods and maintain their state, things got more serious.

3.3 Framing patterns

Image by: Johny Caspari on unsplash

As we have seen, the brain likes to simplify to make things manageable. One of the tools it uses to do that is to place boundaries on ideas, things

Some common patterns

events etc. The resulting framing patterns can then be applied to make sense of experience. There are four basic variants to think about.

3.3.1 Constraint

Here we apply the frame as a 'bouncer' to our thoughts, only allowing in those things that conform with our pattern. In essence, this is sticking our fingers in our ears in order not to hear or acknowledge the unwelcome news.

3.3.2 Single perspective

We use a frame to assess the world of 'other'. We will tend to trust things in frame over things out of frame. Recall the adage: to everyone with a hammer, every problem looks like a nail. Actions follow interpretation, which is shaped by frame of reference.

3.3.3 Discounting

Because we have accepted our frame, we trust it. Therefore, we actively discount anything which does not conform with our frame of reference. So, where Constraint simply ignores problematic data, Discounting explicitly rejects the data. In more extreme cases, we can slip into actively seeking out opportunities to discount non-conforming information. The long-running debate on evolution is replete with examples of those with a fundamentalist frame of reference attacking the theory.

3.3.4 Confirmation

Here, we take data and mould them to conform with our frame of reference. I almost called this pattern 'convolution' because of the lengths we will sometimes go to in order to reshape the world to meet our perspective. Sometimes the result is sublime – I refer you to pretty much any episode of Blackadder justifying his actions; or, for that matter, a Line of Duty interview led by the resolute Superintendent Hastings. However, most of the time, confirmation is not so impressive. What may be shocking to us is just how far we can go in order distort information to satisfy our needs.

Curiously, the effort that may be required to confirm new data may only serve to reinforce our attachment to our frame of reference. The driver seems to be that we reach a point when we are in so deep, that the only sensible thing to do is to keep on digging. Reading these lines now we can see the absurdity of such a cycle of behaviour, yet, we will still find it difficult to resist doing it anyway when we find ourselves in the thick of things.

3.3.5 The good and the bad of framing patterns

Used well, framing patterns speed up analysis and can quickly highlight anomalies. In healthy conditions, this paves the way for learning and change. The hypothesis technique used by some management consultants, for example, frames a problem to facilitate analysis. This can help organisations swiftly and dramatically improve performance by highlighting gaps, inconsistencies, errors etc.

Framing patterns can be unhelpful when they blinker us to what is – or indeed could be – or when they are built on error and so drive inappropriate action. They can entrench prejudices in how we operate. Some of these may, for example, be self-defeating frames of the type: 'I'm not good enough for ...'

Framing patterns can also be a source of anger and outrage. If we have committed to a particular frame of reference, any challenge to that frame can feel like a deeply personal attack. We can leap to defend a frame, even when it's wrong. Worse still, sometimes, the best form of defence is attack, so we may seek to impose our frame on others, which reduces the scope for constructive engagement.

3.4 Authority patterns

Coin depicting Henry VIII, attributed to Steven Cornelisz van Herwijck. Image: public domain from the Metropolitan Museum of Modern Art

The running theme here is how we may assign authority to particular people, things or circumstances and extend the influence of an authority beyond its normal capacity. Again, we have several types to consider.

3.4.1 Cult of the hero

In this scenario, we may attach to a given personality for their politics, their fame, or their specific talent. We then give undue weight to everything they say, without question. For example, consider a popstar talking about a political issue, proportional representation, let's say. They may have the right credentials to talk about this and you can see why they would want to make use of their platform to further their message. However, we would do better to judge their political credibility on their political credentials and the strength of their argument, *not* on the basis that they've had three top 10 hits in the last year.

3.4.2 Bandwagon

This is all about going with the (dominant) majority. This often starts with one dominant personality and then builds into a dominant group. This pattern works in part because we like to belong and there is risk in standing alone: when the mob says 'run', it can be difficult to resist. The effect may be relatively genteel, such as the way in which advertising people refer to percentages of population who really prefer product X. However, there have been multiple experiments illustrating the power of peer pressure.

Perhaps one of the more famous illustrations of peer pressure is the set of Asch experiments. Subjects (who knew nothing about the experiment) were placed in a room with others who did know the experiment's true purpose. Everyone was asked to declare which was the longer/longest line from a selection. Those in on the experiment would then choose the same *incorrect* response. The question then was: how would the experiment's real subjects (those who were not in the know) behave? A surprising number of them went along with the group, even if they had doubts about the claimed correct answer.

Subsequently, there has been heated debate about the details and reliability of the experiment. It does nonetheless seem to capture a phenomenon most of us have observed – and may even admit we have succumbed to on occasion.

In business, the bandwagon often manifests itself as groupthink, where the whole board, design team or project team get behind that one 'killer idea' without having adequately considered the pros and cons.

3.4.3 Availability

The focus here is about assigning (disproportionate) value/ authority to what we have – especially in terms of information. Again, this is not a new phenomenon – think of the proverb 'a bird in the hand is worth two in the bush'. The phrase neatly captures why the pattern is attractive: there is an obvious value to something real, now, rather than just the prospect of something later on.

Let's translate this pattern into a business environment. Consider boards or management teams trying to get to grips with key performance indicators and quarterly or annual reports. These groups do have a lot of data to process and often difficult decisions to make. There should be no surprise, then, that they tend to welcome things that, on the face of it, make their life easier by reducing the volume of data to consider. But they may quickly start to judge all organisational activity solely in the light of their management scorecard. This, in turn, places even more importance on which data are selected and how valid they are.

3.4.4 Anchoring

With this pattern, the focus lands on the first input we have – we then judge all subsequent input in relation to that. This can be a handy tool for calibrating and assessing relative value.

Out in the world, this pattern underlines why, for decades now, we are regularly bombarded by advertising detailing variants on: 'Normal price – ouch. This sale price – a bargain!'. This style of promotional campaign keeps happening because the pattern resonates with enough potential customers to make it worthwhile.

A slightly more sophisticated variant of this pattern is the so-called Goldilocks effect. Faced with three price points on a list (e.g. wine in a restaurant), we will tend towards the middle value. This is because the midpoint suggests that we are being neither cheap nor flash, so feels like a safe place. That said, look closely the next time you are dealing with a choice like this to check whether that 'midpoint' bottle really is at the midpoint price in hard cash terms.

3.4.5 The good and the bad of authority patterns

As with the other examples here, authority patterns have their value. Given what we have seen about the brain's potential fallibility, an appeal to appropriate authorities seems healthy. Alignment with authority also tends to support our sense of belonging – we can be part of 'us' rather than one of 'them'. Used well, external referencing also helps us compare our thinking and reasoning with that of others.

Authority patterns can lead us into unhelpful places though. We like to feel reassured, but, when we are, we don't always test the validity, reliability or accuracy of our chosen authority. If we're not doing this, we run the risk of using judgements that are not valid (i.e. that do not correctly explain or illustrate the issue at hand), nor sufficiently representative, or that are just simply incorrect.

Authority patterns can also tend to discourage innovation and imaginative thinking. Given the importance of innovation in modern business, we might suspect that an unthinking reliance on authority could easily create a serious gap in individual and organisational competence.

A particular modern variant of the authority pattern is the appeal to the Internet and the so-called 'wisdom of crowds'. We may attribute to the crowd some form of deliberate insight into what is being said. But actually, wisdom of crowds is, by and large, by large a statistical, not a noetic phenomenon: there is no collective mental effort, nor is the crowd mystically generating enlightenment. The point is that, with a large enough data sample, we start to produce a reliable map of the averages (be it mode, median or mean) and distribution of whatever is being measured (e.g. customer preferences). The results may be fantastically useful for sales, marketing, PR types etc. That is, of course, provided we can trust the results or understand the margin of error. When we blindly rely on such data, we are as likely to be undermined by the folly of the masses as guided by the wisdom of crowds.

3.5 Overconfidence patterns

Overconfidence can be risky

We have a cluster of patterns that readily get us into trouble: all of them about overconfidence.

3.5.1 Distorted valuation

We tend to overestimate our abilities. In particular, we are too ready to make the leap from little skill to great competence in our assessment of what we can do. The distinction I draw here is:

- A skill is the knowledge and ability to operate a given process. It doesn't matter whether that is an assembly-line skill or the ability to use a processing tool, such as MS Excel.

- Competence, on the other hand, is the ability to understand how to tailor and apply one or more skills appropriately in a variety of situations.

Both may be improved by practice, but, in the end, it is competence that will deliver greater value to the individual and the organisation.

A rather pointed example of this distorted valuation pattern is known as the Dunning-Kruger effect. This has become a bit of a You Tube favourite. The effect sets out to explain how the accuracy of our self-assessment varies over competence. The effect highlights someone whose skill/competence is so low that they cannot understand just how unskilled/incompetent they are. They actually believe they are pretty good. As a meme, this offers scope for much humour, but if we place this pattern into the operating theatre or a building site, that might give us all rather more pause for thought.

3.5.2 Transferability

In the world of HR and employment there is a lot of focus on the so-called transferable skills. Knowing and developing our transferable skills is central to career development. This is especially important as many of the transferable skills tend to be the so-called 'soft skills': rapport building, communication etc.

The fun starts with transferability when we begin to muddle up what is transferable and what is not. We can then end up persuading ourselves that since we are good at accountancy for example, we must already be an effective project manager. Or that, since we are good at circuit design, we are clearly ready to act as CXO of a major tech company.

It is clear that over a lifetime we can acquire, grow and leave behind many skills/competences. Each new learning path, however, is a start from somewhere back towards the bottom, rather than a logic-defying leap from the top of one mountain to another.

3.5.3 The good and bad of overconfidence patterns

In English society in particular there is a slight mistrust of overconfidence, but we all need a bit of it at least. A lot of life is risky. Without believing that we can go further than where we are, we might not prosper at all at work, in love or with friends. So, we need that sense of 'yes we can', even despite the evidence, in order to make that move.

A bit of overconfidence can also turn out to have an unexpected impact on motivation. Once we have publicly said 'we can do it', that tends to create a sense of obligation and thus motivation to get it done, if only to avoid embarrassing ourselves.

On the other hand, a reckless level of overconfidence will tend to lead us to create a vicious downward spiral and so to crash and burn. If our failure means that we start to lose credibility, overconfidence can undermine our ability to engage with others effectively. Further, to be consistent with our claims, we might develop a tendency to ignore our own failings (leading to more crashes, more loss of credibility) and to blame others when things go wrong.

3.6 Tied patterns – the building blocks of personality assessment

Image by: Gregory Maxwell on wiki commons

Some patterns seem to be tied together, such that:

- ☐ If we use pattern X we tend to use pattern Y (let's call these Type A tied patterns), or
- ☐ We tend to use pattern X instead of pattern Y (let's call these Type B tied patterns).

Tied patterns are prevalent in the world of personality assessment, where patterns are clustered together into Type A groupings and then typically paired to create Type B scales. The majority of tools and techniques draw on the same pool of theory and application. The main differences between the tools tend to be in:

- The details of which patterns are allocated to which cluster.

- Whether the clusters are then treated as indicative (preferences) or predictive (traits).

At this stage of our conversation, the point to note is that the more common clusters do seem to capture a useful representation of patterns in action. In particular, they capture something of the experience of multiple patterns working together. We consider here just a few examples of Type B pattern scales (using pattern X instead of pattern Y). Note that:

- The examples that follow borrow from different models, so you will see some overlap in the clusters of patterns shown.

- The positives of the patterns are shown, but not the risks. As a rough rule of thumb, in each set of Type B scales, the blind spots/potential weaknesses of someone drawn to one end of the scale tend to be that they may lack the strengths set out in the cluster at the other end of the scale. So, for example, if you tend to favour Towards patterns (see below), you may struggle with deadlines and spotting risks/problems.

3.6.1 Direction

The two tied Type A groupings here are *Towards* patterns and *Away From* patterns.

- *Towards* patterns tend to include: being goal driven; valuing benefits; being good at identifying and repeating causal patterns that appear successful.

- *Away From* patterns tend to include: being deadline driven; valuing risk avoidance, being good at spotting risks and problems.

Just to underline a further point here, I trust you can see how both patterns could be useful in running a project or organisation. This holds true for all tied pattern clusters.

3.6.2 Scope

The groupings here are around *Conceptual* and *Tangible*.

- *Conceptual* patterns tend to include: big-picture, holistic thinking; seeing the (potential) relationships between things; top-down thinking.
- *Tangible* patterns tend to include: practical thinking/hands-on engagement; attention to the order and detail of things; bottom-up thinking.

3.6.3 Time

The groupings here are about positioning *Through Time* or *In Time*.

- *Through Time* patterns may be past or future focused (the point is they are not focused on 'now'). Through Time patterns tend to include: a keen sense that time is passing by; and as a result, a tendency to be punctual (and expect it in others); planning; filtering dialogue through a past/future focus.
- *In Time* patterns tend to include: spontaneity; being in the moment; ready to make decisions; good at seeing what *is* rather than what *ifs*.

3.6.4 Information focus

The groupings in this scale are *Fact Focus* and *People Focus*.

- *Fact Focus* patterns tend to include: an ability to see and work with the data; being comfortable with processes; led by logical argument.
- *People Focus* patterns tend to include: an ability to work and connect with people; comfortable managing relationships; led by emotional dynamics.

3.6.5 Analysis

The tied groupings here are *Same and Different*.

- *Same* patterns tend to include: being good at spotting patterns; referencing back to experience; a preference for the status quo, especially if it appears to work.
- *Different* patterns tend to include: being good at spotting novelty/anomalies; appealing to possibility; a preference for change and innovation.

3.6.6 The good and bad of tied patterns

Most of us will find that we do tend towards one end of a tied pattern scale more than the other. In the context of personality assessments, most of us will recognise a profile of our set of preferred/espoused patterns. This usually includes some thoughts on how the patterns combine in practice to influence our thinking and choices.

There is no right, wrong nor better profile. But some profiles might be more readily suited to some circumstances. If we linger in environments that conflict with our personality patterns, we can start to feel exasperated, exhausted or lose confidence and motivation. Knowing our patterns can help us manage our day to day lives better. Understanding our own and others' positioning might also help us see how to make our teams more connected and effective.

Key takeaways

- ☐ The brain seems to create an endless variety of patterns – though many appear to be common to most of us.

- ☐ Storytelling, the desire to find a connected narrative in what we experience, may be one of our most fundamental patterns.

- ☐ Causal patterns focus on the story that A can cause B. These patterns can help us see useful connections. But they can also encourage us to mistake correlation for cause.

- ☐ We use Framing patterns to filter out conflicting and other information. But that sometimes means we filter out inconvenient or unwanted information.

- ☐ Authority patterns encourage us to look to an authority for leadership. But if we do this unquestioningly, it can lead us into hot water.

- ☐ Overconfidence patterns can help us do amazing, unexpected things – or fail spectacularly!

- ☐ Tied patterns bring clusters of patterns together and frequently underpin personality assessments that can help inform and improve how teams work together.

4.
Beliefs, values and drivers

There are some special types of pattern that actively shape how we think and act. They tend to be deep-rooted and slow to change. In the coaching context especially, these patterns make regular appearances when coachees are trying to understand their challenges and how to change their circumstances. These patterns are:

- Beliefs: representing ideas about ourselves, others and just about anything as true.

- Values: judgements that we think are so important that we use them to assess the value of actions, outcomes, people. For Rokeach (1973), values can be thought of as:

    - *Instrumental* – they bring about a state we want, or

    - *Terminal* – they represent a key life outcome/end state we want.

    We tend to approve, pursue and promote those values we hold for ourselves.

- Drivers: qualities we think are so important that we use them to guide our attitudes and actions.

4.1 Beliefs

We are perhaps more used to thinking about beliefs in the context of politics and religion. However, they are more pervasive than that. If we think back to the cognitive cycle, the judgement phase assigns one or

Beliefs, values and drivers

multiple characteristics to aspects of an experience. Where experiences reinforce judgements, judgements shift from a 'view', to knowledge, to belief. Beliefs may then act rather like framing patterns, but tend to be more powerful and broader in scope.

Beliefs may be positive or negative – and have a positive or negative impact. Let's take a simple example. In keeping with the spirit of the New Year, we may resolve to improve our fitness. We know that a challenging goal is supposed to be motivating, so why don't we take on a real challenge and run a marathon? We are likely to hold one of several beliefs about doing that:

```
         Qualifying        +      Enabling

      'I can't simply          'I can build up
      start running 26         to running a
      miles a day              marathon in a
      tomorrow'                year'
                                                    +
  -  ─────────────────────┼─────────────────────
                                            Belief

      'I can't get fit         'I can simply
      enough to run            add training to
      a marathon'              my daily
                               routine'

         Limiting          -      Risky
```

So, we might characterise four types of belief:

- ☐ Enabling. Both *belief* and *effect* are positive. We recognise the good sense and potential long-term value of building up our ability to do a marathon at some point in the future.

- ☐ Risky. Here the belief is positive but the effect is negative. A typical view on a New Year's resolution is that we can simply add it to our daily list of things to do. But, actually, as we all know, real change requires more than a bit of diary management. In practical terms for this example, we understand how quickly we might lose the motivation to keep trying to fit our training programme into the existing day.

55

- ☐ Qualifying. Here the belief is negative, but the effect may be positive. We recognise that getting from where we are to being able to run a marathon is something we cannot do alone. With this insight, however, we are then released to make the choice to seek appropriate help; and so improve our chances of achieving our goal.

- ☐ Limiting. Here both the belief and the effect are negative. When we 'know' that we will never be able to do it, then what's the point of even trying?

One key thing to note is that one belief will frame a whole series of actions (or in some cases inactions) and consequences. A belief can spread its influence, a bit like a virus. The limiting belief that we could never do a marathon too easily adds other fitness activities to the 'can't do' list. If we buy into the idea that only very fit people succeed, that same limiting belief can start to eat at our motivation to succeed… and so on.

Again, we need to remember that any negative belief will have started out as the brain's attempting to protect us from a perceived threat/risk. However, as we travel further along the narrative framed by our belief, we move further and further away from the original belief and our understanding of whence it came. Ultimately, there is a good chance that we will lose sight altogether of the belief that led to our decision and its impact on where we now find ourselves. We start to accept and work within the limit we've imposed – and suffer the consequences of that – but without understanding how or why. If we want to change, it is much harder to fight an opponent we cannot see.

Perhaps inevitably, the beliefs we form in childhood are likely to be the most entrenched and enduring beliefs we hold. As adults, we are likely to have forgotten the childhood origins of many of these beliefs. As a result, especially when dealing with limiting beliefs, we may find it harder to accept that these are patterns *we* created; and that these are patterns we can *recreate* or even *replace*. This can make change a serious and unsettling challenge for many of us.

4.2 Values

A strongly held belief about how the world should/could be can manifest as a value: a useful/important principle or standard. There is quite a range of models and lists of potential 'values' to consider, though there seems to be a clear overlap between many of them. To that extent, one list seems as helpful a discussion point as another. That said, the additional distinction between terminal (end) and instrumental (means) values (Rokeach, 1973) helpfully implies different energies and intents.

Similarly, a distinction between personal, central and social values (Gouveia et al, 2013) also seems helpful in that it points to internalised and externalised value positions. This seems a sensible reflection of the idea that values come from external experience and influences as well as internal judgement. It also recognises the possibility of values espoused (for the sake of belonging or at least apparent compliance) and values in practice (what actually matters to us).

We seem to talk a lot about values these days. They feature prominently in most organisations' corporate material, or indeed in the literature of political groupings. We might then assume that we are all clear about what we mean. At the individual (never mind organisational) level, though, it may be surprising to see how many of us are not that certain about the nature, validity and implications of our values.

Indeed, many of us can experience difficulty 'living our values' (Brown, 2018) and be undermined by the conflict between others' expectations of our values and what we actually hold dear. Certainly, that particular conflict has featured in many of the coaching engagements I have had over the years, especially where the values of coachees and their organisations diverge.

Taking a step back, it strikes me how we might characterise much of the values language in terms of our need for security, esteem, or belonging … i.e. reflecting our hierarchy of needs (Maslow, 1954). Seen in the light of Maslow's model, values reflect what needs we are seeking to satisfy (terminal values) and how we get there (instrumental values).

While individual values lists may contain terms that don't quite map neatly to the hierarchy, there seems to be sufficient overlap to merit further examination.

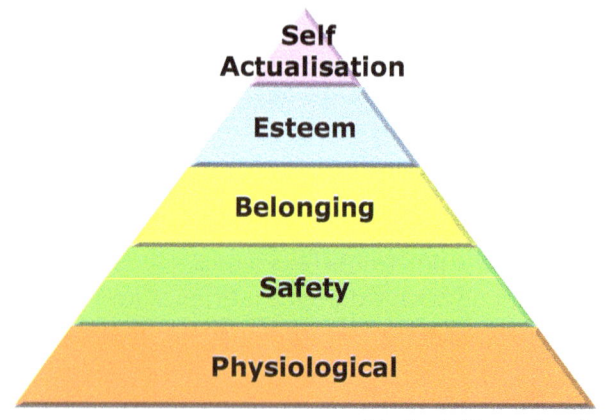

Maslow's Hierarchy of needs (1954)

Values lists can run from a couple of dozen, to hundreds of terms. In practice, most of us will not hold so many in our subconscious, never mind our conscious engagement with the world. We will tend to prioritise the things we will care about. I'd suggest that (perceived) risk/threat is probably the stronger motivation here: if needs are being met, do we worry about them in the same way as we fret about a gap? It is the 'unsatisfied need that motivates' (Covey, 1989).

As a species, we do also seem to be susceptible to 'loss aversion' (Kahneman and Tversky, 1979): our emotional response to loss seems to be stronger than our response to gain. It would follow, then, that we are more likely to prioritise those values reflecting needs that we perceive as under threat.

4.3 Drivers

In the context of this discussion, Transactional Analysis (TA – Stewart and Joines, 2012) suggests the notion of Drivers. In particular, TA identifies 5: be perfect, be strong, try hard, please others, hurry up.

These Drivers are priorities for action and propel internal *scripts* (as in a predefined scene to play out) about what (and how) we should be(come). In the context of this discussion about needs and values, Drivers begin to look rather like instrumental values intended to realise our priority terminal values. Again, there is not a complete one-to-one mapping here, but it is easy to see how we might conclude that 'try hard' is a route to happiness, recognition etc., or that 'please others' might deliver belonging or security.

On the face of it, there should be a strong relationship between beliefs, values and drivers: beliefs should shape values, drivers should impel us to actions and outcomes aligned to our values and beliefs. In practice, it does not seem to be so simple. Beliefs themselves can be tricky things. Values, meanwhile, may prove difficult to define clearly, especially if internal and external values are competing for our allegiance.

Because beliefs, values and drivers are so ingrained, they can be difficult to shift. Indeed, even conflicting experience can find itself marshalled to reinforce a belief, so:

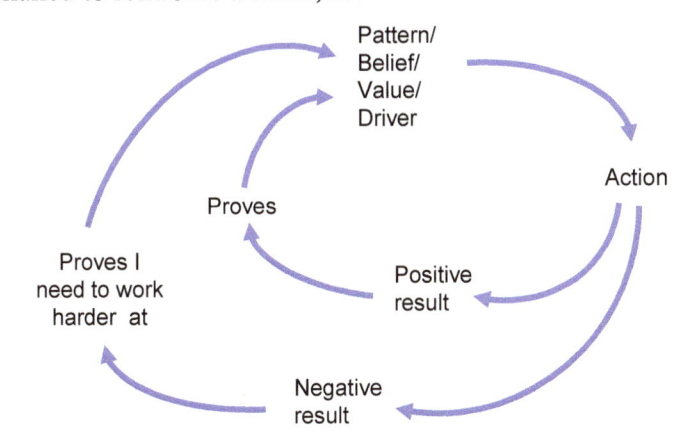

Recall the confirmation pattern we discussed earlier. One potential unhappy consequence of patterns is that risky and counter-productive beliefs etc. may be continually reinforced. In turn, this consolidates our attachment to beliefs, values and drivers that may not deliver, may impair our efforts, or may just be downright harmful. By the way, finding validating proof of our beliefs etc. tends to trigger the 'reward' neurotransmitters. In other words, actions reinforcing our beliefs etc. are rewarded at the biological level. Inevitably, the brain will be drawn towards (and potentially addicted to) actions that spark that 'feel good' moment.

4.4 A final word on patterns

We have spent quite a bit of time on patterns, some common patterns and the special patterns that become beliefs, values and drivers. My emphasis reflects both the importance and the prevalence of patterns in all their nature and complexity for the way that the brain copes with everything that's out there. Patterns matter because they are phenomenally helpful tools. But, we need to recognise that patterns are not always our friends. When it comes to being consciously in control of our own destiny, patterns may simply get in the way. If we want to make conscious, active choices about where we are headed and how, then we need to learn to work with patterns rather than just succumb to them.

Beliefs, values and drivers

Key takeaways

- There are special types of pattern that actively shape our perception and decisions across a whole range of behaviours. These are beliefs, values and drivers.

- Beliefs are fundamental patterns that influence (sometimes even infect) large areas of our world view. Beliefs can be enabling, risky, qualifying or limiting. Because beliefs are so deep-rooted, it can be difficult for us to spot beliefs at work in our thinking.

- Values express principles and standards important to us and seem to reflect our deepest needs. But we are not always as clear as we think we are about what really matters – and this can lead to conflicts of values at work and elsewhere.

- Drivers impel us towards actions and outcomes that help realise our values and goals.

- Beliefs, values and drivers are so powerful that they encourage confirmation thinking – negative feedback only confirms the need to work harder to satisfy our belief.

- For all their power, beliefs, values and drivers can be changed.

- If we want to own our destiny, we need to work with our patterns, rather than simply succumb to them.

5
Errors in the machine

If the brain's processes and short-cuts were not complicated enough, they also turn out to be less than perfect. The 'machine' gets it wrong with or without external encouragement. We are still learning how exactly the brain works (and fails), which makes it difficult to be precise or accurate about just how well the brain does things.

If we think about it, most of us are happy with and heartily approve of any machine operating with accuracy above 90%. Indeed, at this level, failure is already so unexpected that it can land as a minor disaster (when we lose that computer file, the phone battery dies, the last train is cancelled … I could go on, but we all know the pain). So, with something operating with, say, 99% accuracy, we would probably call that perfect for practical purposes. But, here is the thing:

> *If the brain is conducting the equivalent of something like 100zettaflop actions a day, then, even if it is accurate to 1 trillionth of a percent, that still means it is making about 1 billion errors a day.*

Now, these numbers are to illustrate a point. We simply don't know exactly how accurate our brains are. But we do know that we make mistakes, so we have to be mindful of the fact that our brains are not perfect machines. The figure above serves to underline that even a miniscule level of inaccuracy will produce a lot of errors every day. Most of those errors will be inconsequential, but some will matter and, if they feed into our patterns, will have a lasting effect.

For the most part, brain errors will happen deep down in our subconscious, so we will not see the resulting glitch in the system, which then becomes a glitch in how we think. In our ignorance, we happily carry on assuming and acting as if we are right. A lot of the time, this will not matter – but some errors will be significant. There are three main sources of error to be aware of: physical effects, user error and errors of influence.

5.1 Physical effects

Clearly, injury or illness and disease can take their toll on the brain's ability to operate. Understanding these issues, however, would take us deep into a world of psychology, medicine, neuroscience and therapeutic practice far beyond the scope of this discussion. So, for now, we simply note that these factors may damage part or all of the cognitive cycle. This may result in disruption to our ability to:

- ☐ Assess the situation
- ☐ Create new memories
- ☐ Recall memories, or
- ☐ Apply our past experience in a meaningful way to what may come.

The brain's habit of specialisation may make it particularly vulnerable to injury, illness or disease. The brain does have tremendous powers of recovery from damage that can help us carry on, which means it can often, though not always, compensate for damage over time.

In the normal course of things, the brain functions as expected. We do need to remember, however, that the brain spends its life bathing in something of a chemical soup which is in constant flux. This flux adds further uncertainty to the gargantuan undertaking that is the brain's daily work. Stress, mental health problems and similar factors can dramatically alter the chemical balance, which in turn affects brain performance. We have also seen that simply operating at such high levels of activity incurs the risk of multiple errors each day. Some of these will be unnoticeable. Some may introduce unhelpful glitches into our cognitive cycle and the way a pattern develops.

5.2 User error

While the cognitive cycle seems simple and stable, we have seen that emotion can shape our assessment of an event. The flows and counter flows of stress, love, anger, fear and joy can directly shape our actions and how we understand the world. In other words, emotion moulds the cognitive cycle, the creation of memories and the development and application of patterns.

Unhelpfully, it seems to be the strength of an emotion rather than its relevance that matters. Thus, the bad mood that we bring to a meeting caused by having become rain-soaked on the way to work starts to colour our mood, but also our appreciation of the meeting. All too quickly, that mood affects our judgement on the people we are meeting. It does not take many steps to move from 'I had a difficult meeting with X today' to 'I hate having meetings with X – they are so difficult'. Fans of team sports may have noticed how the testing behaviour of one team member may begin to create a negative thought pattern in the mind of the referee: penalties and other censure against the whole team may soon follow.

The brain's habit of approximation can also play its part in creating errors. Approximation works because, in the moment, it tends to be good enough. Of course, the working assumption here is that we have approximated correctly. By skipping some detail for the sake of short-term convenience, we may inadvertently be creating errors in emerging patterns. By the time the pattern is established, those errors, if we were ever aware of them, may be long forgotten.

5.3 Errors of influence

As we have seen, memory is malleable – in what we remember and how we remember when creating a memory; and in what we subsequently recall. We have already seen some examples of authority patterns (dominant personality, the bandwagon) and how they may influence the brain's processes. It is a small step from there (as per the

Asch experiments we discussed earlier) to seeking actively to mould another person's thoughts or patterns (including beliefs, values and so on).

When it comes to influencing others, suggestion (either before or after the event) turns out to be a much more powerful tool than we might have imagined. We see it – sometimes even experience it – in any magic show. Suggestion is also to be found in areas of government strategy. In several instances, Western governments this millennium have adopted the use of so-called 'nudge' techniques in order to encourage behaviours in target populations. Simple shifts in communication have been shown to have significant impact on e.g. job seeker behaviour. Continuing investment in these techniques seems like clear evidence of their positive effect.

We tend to think of suggestion as being about language. In fact, multiple senses are regularly targeted to achieve influence. Visual clues tend to be the most obvious, yet at the same time most overlooked form of suggestion. This may be as simple as signs encouraging us to walk on the left or wait on the right. Supermarkets, meanwhile, subtly place goods in their aisles to increase the probability that we will spend more time looking at those particular goods (and, the sales team hopes, buy them).

For one particularly vivid example of suggestion at work, consider what happened at Schiphol airport in The Netherlands. In the 1990s, management at the airport ran an interesting experiment. They placed an image of a fly on the men's urinals, intended to encourage men to aim more effectively and improve hygiene. The results were impressive: 80% reduction in 'spillage' and 8% reduction in cleaning costs. This simple measure generated tangible hygiene, economic and environmental benefits. For obvious reasons, the idea has been picked up elsewhere.

Equally, scents (warm bread in a house up for sale, or bacon wafting out of the breakfast café that is about to open) can directly change our perception, evoke positive memories and invite our positive association.

Sound, and in particular music, is another especially potent key. You may have noticed, for example, the great majority of us all adore exactly the same music: the music that we were most attached to during our teenage years. The combination of sound, energy, hormones and emotion is just too intoxicating. Not surprisingly, music associated with key life moments then comes a close second in our enduring memory.

Although we notice some sound effects, we may not always be so aware of the role music and sound play in, say, the cinema. Watch Jaws with the sound turned down and you might be forgiven for the occasional chuckle at the dated, albeit very large, rubber fish. Watch it with the sound as intended and most people will manage at least a brief doublecheck before stepping into their bath over the following few days!

5.4 The truth is out there

There is no question that our brains do a brilliant job for us, all day, every day. However, we have seen already that our brain is contending with representations of the world out there, rather seeing exactly what is. Moreover, our magnificent brains are capable of getting things wrong on their own, as well as thanks to external influences. Worse still, we may not realise that a fault exists. Recognising the potential for error should give us pause for thought about some of our certainties.

One particular challenge is how we deal with the matter of truth. If the brain is constrained to working with representations of 'other', then getting at *what is* can be pretty tricky. Our brains are kept at a remove from reality and must battle to understand it from within the biochemical processes and patterns that shape our thinking. Clearly, we run a major risk of becoming trapped in our own bubble, trapped by our own limiting beliefs. Things *can* get better if we seek multiple perspectives to help compensate for our own limitations. So, 'I' must go out there, out to 'other', in order to home in on the truth.

Even with the help of a variety of people, getting at the truth can be a difficult job. For example, the phenomenon known as the Rashomon effect shows how difficult arriving at even simple agreement can be. The name comes from a film which focused on the testimony of multiple witnesses to the same event. Not only did the accounts not match, but, in some key respects, various accounts were plainly at odds with each other. For our purposes, it does not matter whether the differences were accidental or deliberate – after all, we often don't know in real life.

If the truth matters, then we are going to have to work at it. For some, the challenge collapses into the notion that since our perception is the only thing we can know, then in effect we must accept this ('my truth') as *the* truth. This is a tempting and potentially comforting approach, but clearly flawed thinking. Moreover, it does not inevitably follow that because something is difficult, it is impossible.

The challenge then is how, given our brilliant but imperfect resources, we can arrive at truths that help us build understanding and progress. In the end, that can only be by building a consensus based on evidence and testing (as rigorous as that needs to be). Getting there may involve effort, time and quite a bit of frustration (who hasn't at least once cried out, if only to themselves: 'why can't they see the right answer?'). That, in turn, has implications for how we engage and communicate with, listen to and learn from others.

Over time, such an approach helps build a consensus in which we can have confidence. It also has the advantage of bringing with it a healthy side-serving of better connectivity with others and a better sense of belonging for ourselves.

5.5 The brain's strange universe – again

We have taken a brief look at some of the consequences of how the brain tries to cope with a non-stop flow of data. We've covered quite a lot of ground and some of it – especially the introduction of often fundamental uncertainties – may feel a bit scary. We need to remember that the tricks and habits the brain develops serve it well for most of the time. They can help speed up our assessment of whether something is safe or risky, interesting or dull, or demands action: they help us understand ourselves and the world better.

Precisely because they are successful, we tend to rely on those tricks of the brain – especially patterns – a lot. And that's when the problems are likely to begin. Brains can get it wrong – on their own and with help from others. Patterns may be wrong or misplaced. Shortcuts may have missed key data that seemed trivial at the time. Beyond that, errors (of any flavour) can further distort the brain's workings. As a result, the brain's habits can lead us into mindsets and actions that not only don't serve us well, but actively undermine us. Recognising this risk should give us pause for thought.

In the coaching context, we need to recognise that coachees may be a little shocked when they discover glitches in their thinking. To that extent, part of the coach's role is to help their coachee navigate uncertain waters.

If we want to gain some control of how we think, of the failings in our processes, and make some headway towards truth, we need to work at it. That means building a way of engaging that accepts that 'I' and 'other' need each other, even if their interaction sometimes feels more like conflict than harmony.

Key takeaways

- ☐ Given the sheer volume of daily brain activity, even if it is consistently accurate to a minute degree, the brain is making lots of errors every single day.

- ☐ The majority of brain errors are likely to go unnoticed, even if some of them are significant.

- ☐ Physical effects, including damage and stress are clear causes of error.

- ☐ The patterns our brains create can be flawed, so that we end up doing the 'right thing' at the wrong time and vice versa.

- ☐ The brain's processes are malleable – a fact that sales teams, PR people, politicians and other interest groups all seek to exploit.

- ☐ If the truth matters, then getting at it is something we need to work at. This implies we need to find a way to engage that accepts that 'I' and 'other' both come to the table with limitations - and need each other to move forward.

6
So, how did 'I' get here?

This next section may seem a bit philosophical for a book about the practicalities of the brain and how we better serve our coachees. But the work of coaching always starts and ends with the person, the personality, the 'I' that presents itself. This presenting 'I' is usually looking to change, to improve an aspect of their life, which means that 'I' needs to change. So it makes practical sense for us to have a basic understanding of what 'I' might actually be if we're going to be working with it.

For the most part, we will readily refer to ourselves as 'I', confident in our sense of self as a unique individual, in our sense of our 'personality', in our sense of who and what we are. Our 'I' feels tangible, permanent and reliable, but, as I hope we have seen already, reality is a little more complicated and complex than that.

Once we begin to explore what 'I' is, it can feel like jumping off a cliff edge, blindfolded, at night, as we start to perceive that 'I':

- ☐ Is perhaps not 'a' phenomenon or entity.
- ☐ Might in fact be the product of several 'I's at play in our mind.
- ☐ Is not as reliable as we tend to assume. We know we forget. We know we can get things wrong. We also recognise that we err and forget more than we know.
- ☐ Is not as constant as we assume. We all change and the 'I' of today is not the same 'I' of, say, 10, 5 or even just 2 years ago.
- ☐ Can be difficult to talk about clearly, given that we must do so within the confines of the mind and tools that are part of that thing we think of as 'I'. So, when we try to pin down what 'I' is, it

can all too easily start to feel as though we are trapped in a hall of mirrors.

In practice, 'I' turns out to be more ephemeral, more mercurial, multi-faceted and multi-layered than we tend to believe. We have been debating, wrestling and often just plain arguing about what 'I' might be for millennia now. There does not seem to be an easy or imminent solution to the problem. There are lots of views out there. But let's take a couple of perspectives – the mystical entity and the emergent property – just to highlight some of the challenges. These two examples are deliberately 'opposites' in order to help test our assumptions and get us thinking.

6.1 'I' as mystical entity

The basic notion here is that 'I' is some coherent entity that occupies the human shell. Typically in such arguments, 'I' and body are distinct. From a religious perspective, 'I' often becomes the soul and is something gifted to this world via a human body, before moving on to some other form of existence. The human challenge is then to:

- Discover the true self   and/or
- Develop the self.

This is usually in the context of serving some higher purpose. It is easy to see how this mindset might shape the development of a sense of destiny, in turn shaping beliefs about our role in life, our values and our drivers.

As a model, variations on this theme dominated most civilisations for a very long time. It is easy to see why:

- As an argument, it is quite a strong one, in the sense that it is difficult to prove/disprove; and in that it exists beyond our worldly experience, so appeals to an authority beyond us (and is therefore beyond (re)proof).

- At the individual level, it provides clarity and appears to solve the potentially difficult conversation about 'I', mind and brain.

- The model implies hierarchy (something above/beyond us is in play) which puts us in context. So, even if we do not understand or perceive it, we belong to something. This makes the model inherently comforting.

- Where purpose/destiny is involved, the model can be highly motivating (we have seen already that the mind/brain responds well to a focus/purpose).

- The appeal to a higher authority implies an authority that is watching and as a consequence, we are seen. But, potentially, we may also be held to account for our actions by that authority.

6.2 'I' as emergent property

The concept here sits within the set of ideas holding that biology and evolution can explain all for our social species. Here, the 'I' is not a thing in and of itself. Rather, it grows out of the brain's natural and infinitely repeated functions. 'I', here, is a product of a complex and dynamic system, wherein accrued experiences and judgments crystallise into something affective and self-reflective. The notion of a machine producing personality, or hosting human personality in a computer, is a rich source of inspiration for science fiction. Watching the progress in the design and development of prosthetics controlled by the brain suggests the model is also a rich source of inspiration for science fact.

At first glance, what we think of as 'I' seems too rich and complex to have arrived this way. However, complex dynamic systems are capable of producing surprising results. Consider the image below.

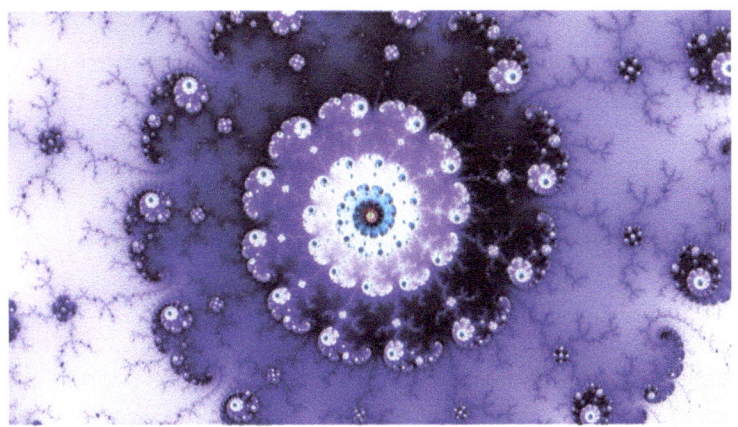

Image by: seriani on wiki commons

We are dipping our toes into the mysterious world of chaos theory and fractals. This is all about the mathematics developed to help understand/map complex dynamic systems that have a number of features. Such systems are:

- Infinitely complex, yet self-similar at different scales
- Driven by recursion
- Based on iteration of a simple process over and over in a feedback loop.

Some of the complex mathematical formulas that came out of chaos theory happened to have an alluring effect when used to generate images, such as the one shown here. The Mandelbrot Set is probably the most famous group of fractal images, but you can readily download free apps to generate your own images too. The point is that a 'simple' set of rules can generate very complex patterns over time.

Let's reflect for a moment on these characteristics and how they relate to what we have seen about the workings of the brain. The brain sounds a lot like the sort of complex, dynamic system that would appeal to students of chaos theory. If the brain's behaviour looks like a complex system, then perhaps its outputs reflect that too.

Critically, the brain's capacity and capability for memory enables the brain to reflect on what it has done. In that respect, memory gives birth to analysis and in turn to self-recognition and development. The brain begins to find meaning in repetition. So, we may find ourselves coming to the view that 'I' is less about *cogito* and more about *itero ergo sum*. In this universe, our sense of good and evil may simply be the product of an infinitely extended series of pleasurable and painful experiences, judgements and memories.

Models in this grouping draw heavily on biology, psychology and, increasingly, neuroscience and are relatively new to the debate about 'I' and self and personality. They are attracting support, not least because:

- ☐ Their strength lies in their increasing ability to draw on reliable and scientifically valid evidence.
- ☐ 'I', mind and brain are joined together as manifestations of a single biology and set of processes.
- ☐ The model does not depend on an external authority in order for 'I' to exist.
- ☐ Without authority or externalised purpose, each 'I' becomes responsible and accountable for itself, what it does and what it becomes.
- ☐ 'I' is alone unless it chooses not to be. Though it must experience 'other' in order to develop (data are needed to feed the process).

For many of us, still, the notion that 'I' is a symptom rather than a cause of repeated engagement with the universe feels challenging. But, for the moment at least, scientific research seems to be building the case for 'I' as an emergent property.

6.3 Magic or complexity?

This was just a brief look at some of the argumentation about what constitutes 'I'. There are others to explore if you're interested. The points to land here are that:

- ☐ I hope you have seen that how we think about who/what we are may have a direct impact on the developing shape of the patterns we use. Some of these patterns will then crystallise as beliefs, values and drivers that shape our behaviour.
- ☐ In our day to day, most of us tend to align to one perspective, to the exclusion of others. This alignment will encourage us to seek out others who appear to be of like belief, so reinforcing the 'rightness' of our position in the first place. At the same time, this increasing assurance serves to distance other perspectives. So our notion of 'I' inevitably shapes the 'we' that we build for and around ourselves.
- ☐ Some patterns in the clusters we adopt are likely to show up in curious ways. Take, for example, the patterns we adopt in relation to our personal authority or responsibility. If our response to magic or complexity is that we have no responsibility, for example, we are more likely to be drawn into risky/unhelpful behaviour.

As I write, no one argument has yet really clinched the debate. In my experience, most of the arguments run into trouble at some point or other. In the end, none of them is entirely satisfying. I think, however, that both coaches and coachees can benefit from understanding something of the complexity of 'I', because in the end, it is a coachee's 'I' that must change for them to secure the changes/improvements they seek. The fact that 'I' is uncertain should remind us that:

- ☐ The coachee journey is therefore uncertain – and potentially intimidating for them because of it.
- ☐ We cannot assume that we each share the same sense of 'I'. Therefore, the coachee route forward may be very different from the one we might envisage for them; or, indeed, that they envisaged for themselves.

6.4 A need to be seen

The curious, elusive and mercurial nature of 'I' may drive what seems to be one of our most fundamental desires: to be seen. Whether 'I' is about purpose or about experience, it is validated and grows through interaction with 'other'. Seeking to be seen means seeking to interact. Experiences of rejection or abandonment in the world out there can only exacerbate and potentially distort the desire to be seen, which may then further affect our behaviour. As Steven Grosz (2013) observed, we may find ourselves astounded at the lengths people will go to 'avoid the catastrophe of indifference'. This may simply manifest as seeking success, power or reward in our chosen paths, but you can see how easily such a need might become counterproductive.

In this context, social media, for all their benefits, create a marvellously effective and compelling *indifference machine*. The sales pitch is that by using social media we can be seen by millions. The reality is that millions are already there and trying to achieve the same outcome. The resulting noise makes it almost impossible to stand out from the crowd. In response, we may feel nudged to step into more and more unnatural and outrageous behaviours in order to draw attention to ourselves. Without conscious action to hold us in check, we know what can happen next:

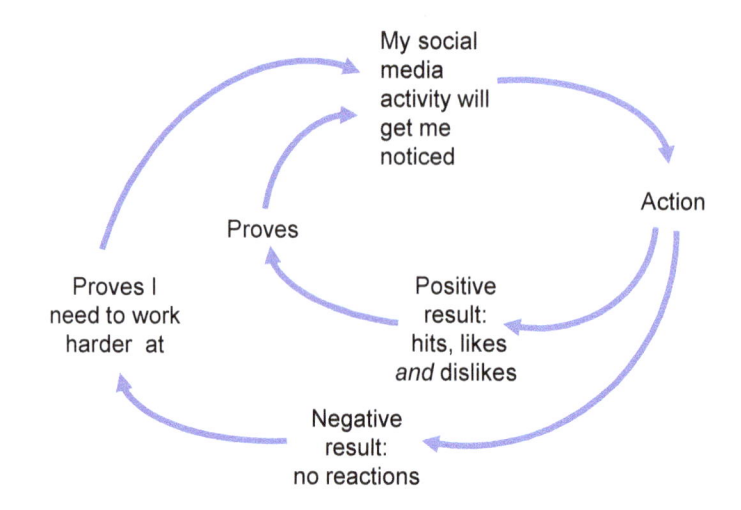

Everybody follows suit. The noise levels go up and on it goes. Note also that dislikes/hostile responses are validating positive results because they confirm we have been seen. Again, remember that validation activates the reward neurotransmitters, enhancing the addictive quality of our behaviour. If we simply leave the patterns in charge, it is difficult to see this experience not ending in exhaustion and dejection for many.

6.5 A question of choice

As I said at the start of this journey, we tend to think of ourselves as reasonably smart, coherent decision makers. I hope by now I've shown that things are less clear cut than that. For good reasons, the brain survives and thrives by using lots of short-cuts that allow quick – and relatively thoughtless – decisions. Most of the time, this behaviour serves us well. It saves time and it allows us space to think about more complex issues.

With headspace to plan, reflect and learn, we have the opportunity to grow and to become so much more than the obvious sum of our biological components. We must, therefore, allow our brains to continue to find short-cuts to help us – that is a key function for us all. However, we also need to recognise that our brains can get in the way. When, for example, it comes to dealing with change or acknowledging error, it seems clear to me that we have so much to gain by taking more (conscious) control of at least some of the choices we make.

6.5.1 Dealing with change

One consequence of the way the brain gives us headspace is that the majority of our actions are guided by patterns, not 'live' thoughts. The patterns in turn are based on, and are then about, reapplying experience: literally about history repeating itself. The current consensus seems to be that we, homo sapiens, have been around for about 300,000 years, in an existence that seemed stable, if under constant threat. That very stability made patterns an effective coping mechanism. However, in the last 300 years, we have seen more change, on a greater scale, than in the previous 300,000 years of our existence. We are told, more or less on a daily basis, that change is the one constant; that it is happening faster than ever; and that there is more of it than ever (!). If all of that is true, then we have to wonder how far we can rely on a mechanism such as patterning, which relies fundamentally on unchanging circumstances to succeed. In our more uncertain age, a more fluid, conscious engagement with our brain might suit us better.

6.5.2 Acknowledging error

We have also seen that there are several sources of potential error in the brain's core cognitive processes. As a result, there may be faults in some of our patterns, including our beliefs, values and drivers, that can have a pervasive and negative influence on how we engage with the world. If our patterns are wrong, there is a fair chance they are leading us in the wrong direction; that they may be adding to our problems rather than providing solutions.

6.5.3 Why making a choice matters

I think one of the key challenges for our imperfect selves in a more complex, dynamic universe is to find a way to continue to exploit the brain's natural efficiency strategies. We need to achieve this at the same time as scaling up the role of our conscious 'I' to validate and, if necessary, redirect our intentions and actions. In other words, it would help us to grow the habit of actively making a choice more often than we do. The balancing act is not an easy one:

- ☐ We have myriad patterns ready to deploy.
- ☐ There is an emotional aspect to all our patterns.
- ☐ We're under constant pressure to be quick (dynamic systems tend to prioritise action over reflection and even accuracy).

- Re-thinking a situation and our response can be hard and energy expensive.
- To re-think is to accept doubt and the possibility of error. To that extent, the activity is a direct challenge to the brain and to 'I'.
- Because our patterns may often be right, it can take time to build the evidence and confidence to do things differently.
- We do not want simply to flip to the majority of our decisions being conscious ones. That would be too exhausting. Rather, we need to find a happy point of trade-off between making more decisions for positive effect and the additional effort that might require.

The balance can be shifted. Those of us who are coaches are privileged to see that the evidence that change is worth the effort is clear for those who make the journey. That's why, for me, making a choice to engage our brains consciously more of the time is a critical step if we want to make genuine progress.

6.6 How did 'I' get here?

Our sense of 'I' seems like a natural, fundamental quality, yet it turns out to be something rather more difficult to pin down. We are not entirely sure what 'I' is – or for that matter where 'here' is. That doesn't stop us from pursuing what we think 'I' wants – even in the face of evidence (of influence, of error, of the wrong patterns of thinking) to the contrary. Given that there is so much uncertainty, we should think about how much we are really willing to delegate to subconscious processes.

Executive/business coaching has been shown to be an effective context/support for those who want to make changes. The next part of this book turns to looking at how what we have seen about the workings of the brain and 'I' can manifest and play out in the coaching experience.

How did 'I' get here?

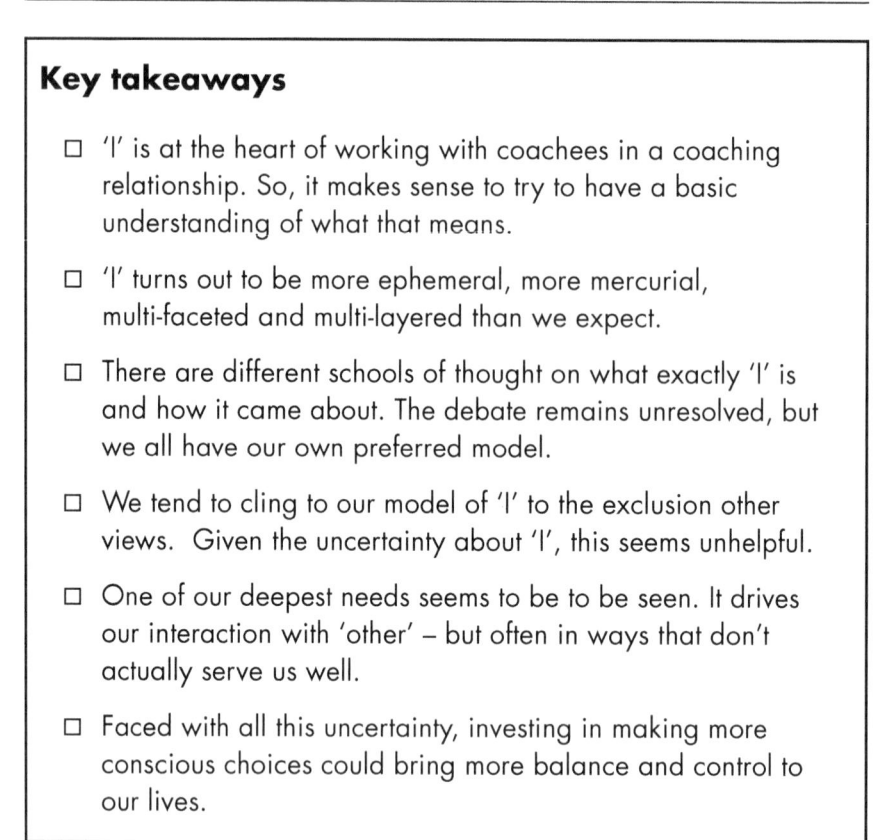

> **Key takeaways**
>
> ☐ 'I' is at the heart of working with coachees in a coaching relationship. So, it makes sense to try to have a basic understanding of what that means.
>
> ☐ 'I' turns out to be more ephemeral, more mercurial, multi-faceted and multi-layered than we expect.
>
> ☐ There are different schools of thought on what exactly 'I' is and how it came about. The debate remains unresolved, but we all have our own preferred model.
>
> ☐ We tend to cling to our model of 'I' to the exclusion other views. Given the uncertainty about 'I', this seems unhelpful.
>
> ☐ One of our deepest needs seems to be to be seen. It drives our interaction with 'other' – but often in ways that don't actually serve us well.
>
> ☐ Faced with all this uncertainty, investing in making more conscious choices could bring more balance and control to our lives.

II

Coaching with 'I' – the coaching landscape

So far, we have been looking at what the brain does to make its work possible – and some of the consequences of those short-cuts in terms of how we interpret the world, our actions and our sense of the 'I' that we assume manages all that activity. We now start to consider the implications of what we have seen for the coaching landscape. With that in mind, we look at:

- The coaching context – the coaching environment turns out to be quite a complex one, with multiple factors to manage (chapter 7).
- Insights from learning and development ideas – which can help coachees structure and consolidate their plans for change (chapter 8).
- The core coaching intentions – expose, explore, evolve – that frame the dialogue (chapter 9).
- Models for talking about the mind (chapter 10). We have seen that this can be challenging. I outline two popular models to help coachees understand and articulate what's going on.
- Coaching focus (chapter 11) explores potential differences between the needs and aspirations of coachees and coaching clients.

All of the themes discussed in this chapter are likely to weave their way through a coaching engagement once underway. I explore them here, before we look at contracting for coaching, because some awareness and sensitivity to the ideas raised can help build a robust and constructive commercial relationship with clients as we move towards a contract. It can also help provide the platform for a strong client relationship. More pointedly, contracting without taking any account of the ideas raised in this section will tend to increase the risk to a coaching contract and coaching relationship. The value isn't just for coaches. Where possible, I try to discuss the ideas with potential coachees or coaching clients, for the simple reason that the better prepared they are for their coaching engagement, the more they tend to get out of it.

As coaches, there is a lot for us to get our head around in this section and the next. The temptation, especially for new coaches wanting to do the right thing, will be to try to do everything perfectly from the start. However, that is not how people are built. It takes time to create and embed good practice and we will make mistakes along the way. The important things are to:

- Seek to do the best by our coachees at each opportunity
- Commit to doing better next time
- Accept and learn from, rather than succumb to the mistakes we make.

7
The coaching context

The primary purpose of coaching is to provide effective and constructive support to a coachee as they seek to explore and develop their potential. In principle, we can do that from:

- A narrow perspective: focusing on the specific situation the coachee wants to change. This can often produce useful quick wins.

- A broader perspective: recognising that the brain's habit of using patterns is likely to lead them to keep creating similar unwelcome situations. Thus, here we not only help our coachees address today's challenge, we help them explore what's driving their situation. That way, we can help them identify and create a more resilient and sustainable solution. Often, the coachee will see new opportunities to change things in other parts of their work or personal life too. This approach does usually require more work, but it's worth it.

Wherever we focus our practice, at the very least we need to be mindful of the broader context in which the coachee operates. As we will see, a coachee exists within a complex 'ecosystem'. When they begin to make changes in one part of the system, that almost invariably has one or more knock-on effects in other areas of their ecosystem. Some effects can be surprising, such that the coachee may need support in resolving those effects with their attempts to change.

Given the impacts coaching may have, we owe it to our coachees to ensure that they understand the potential limits of any quick fixes (narrow perspective) – and of the need for effort if they want to sustain change (broader perspective).

Coaching with 'I' – the coaching landscape

Recall the brain's core cognitive cycle:

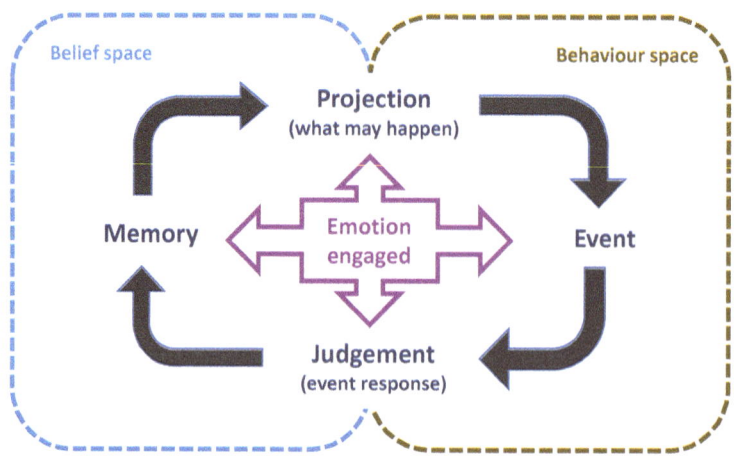

Belief space | **Behaviour space**

- **Projection** (what may happen)
- **Memory**
- **Emotion engaged**
- **Event**
- **Judgement** (event response)

A pattern is not simply about the template, but also about its application and associated actions throughout the cycle. Many patterns and experiences may prove common to us, although each individual coachee arrives with their own highly developed catalogue of experiences, emotions, patterns and clusters of patterns. In general, they are unlikely to be fully aware of all of these facets of their 'personality'. Thus, each coachee brings a different and less than fully conscious mindset/attitude to the challenges they face.

7.1 The inner context

Coachees are likely to have come to coaching with a particular aim in mind. They may or may not be fully aware of the interactions between the context they are working in, their mindset, emotion and behaviour. I think it helpful for a coach to have in mind a basic map of how all of these factors may link up in the coachee's mind. One useful model is the Integrative Relationship Model (IRM) developed by Erdös et al (2020). Given what we have seen about the role of memory (for good and bad), it helps to draw memory explicitly into the model, which gives us a map like this:

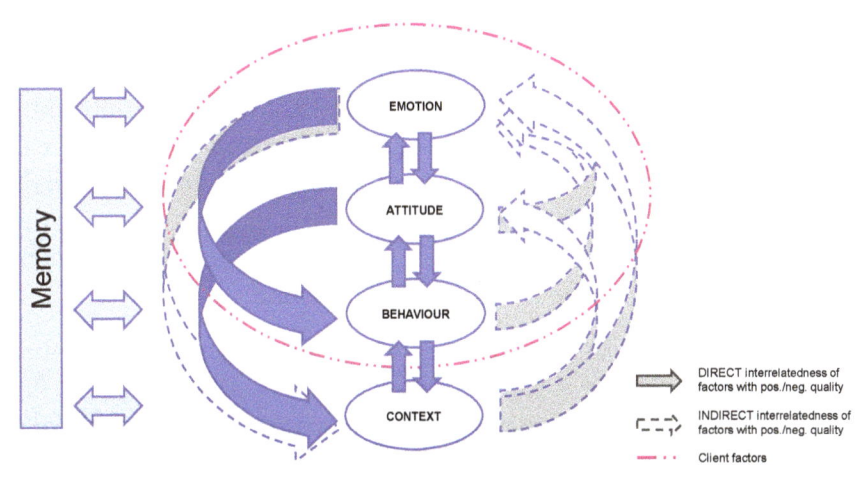

Adapted from Integrative Relationship Model (IRM) (Erdös et al, 2020)

For me, this adapted IRM model helpfully highlights the interactivity of the key factors:

- Attitude – encompassing values, beliefs, drivers and knowledge.
- Behaviour – encompassing skills/competence, behaviour and physiological factors.
- Emotion – recognising that the coachee may not be aware of the emotional charge in their processes. They may also be unaccustomed to discussing the emotional component of their thinking and experience openly with others.
- Context – in a fuller sense. Clearly, the coachee brings not just themselves, but the influence of others (friends, relatives, work colleagues etc.) to their coaching experience.
- Memory – operating as both store and recall processes that shape and are shaped by the other factors.

The IRM feels like a useful starting point for thinking about the coachee's mindset. From the coach's perspective, the basic IRM feels incomplete in that it focuses on the coachee alone. There are at least two human beings 'present' in a coaching session (even if the meeting is a virtual one). Both parties activate and experience the same processes when engaging with other. So what the coach brings to the engagement is in play too. In that sense, the IRM model usefully hints at the phenomena of *transference* and *counter-transference*. This is about the potential tendency of coachee and coach to project their thoughts/feelings on to the other – and often then assume that the other person is thinking/acting in a way consistent with their own projections. Confusion will then not be far behind.

The coachee's mindset can affect the coaching experience in a number of ways. In particular, it can provoke (unexpected) reactions in the coach. From a Transactional Analysis perspective, for example, the coachee's experience may have taught them that stepping into *Child* is generally effective at provoking a *Parent* response. By stepping into Child, they might try to absolve themselves of their own responsibility in and for a situation. The shift invites the other person (in this case, the coach) to step into the role of Parent (and solve their problem for them) as something of a natural response. This urge is inevitably reinforced by a coach's natural desire to help. But a coach drawn into Parent behaviour has stopped coaching. Set down here in black and white, this looks like an obvious trap. However, in the setting of a live coaching session, the shifts can be swift and subtle; and all of this can happen in a moment and without notice.

So, whether we like it or not, the coach's inner context is part of the coaching engagement too. As coaches, we have a professional duty with regard to the coaching relationship. This includes maintaining the appropriate relationship and practising individual reflection and supervision. In other words, we need to be aware of our own context. We therefore need to include the coach in the picture and we then end up with an integrative relationship model for coaching which looks more like:

The coaching context

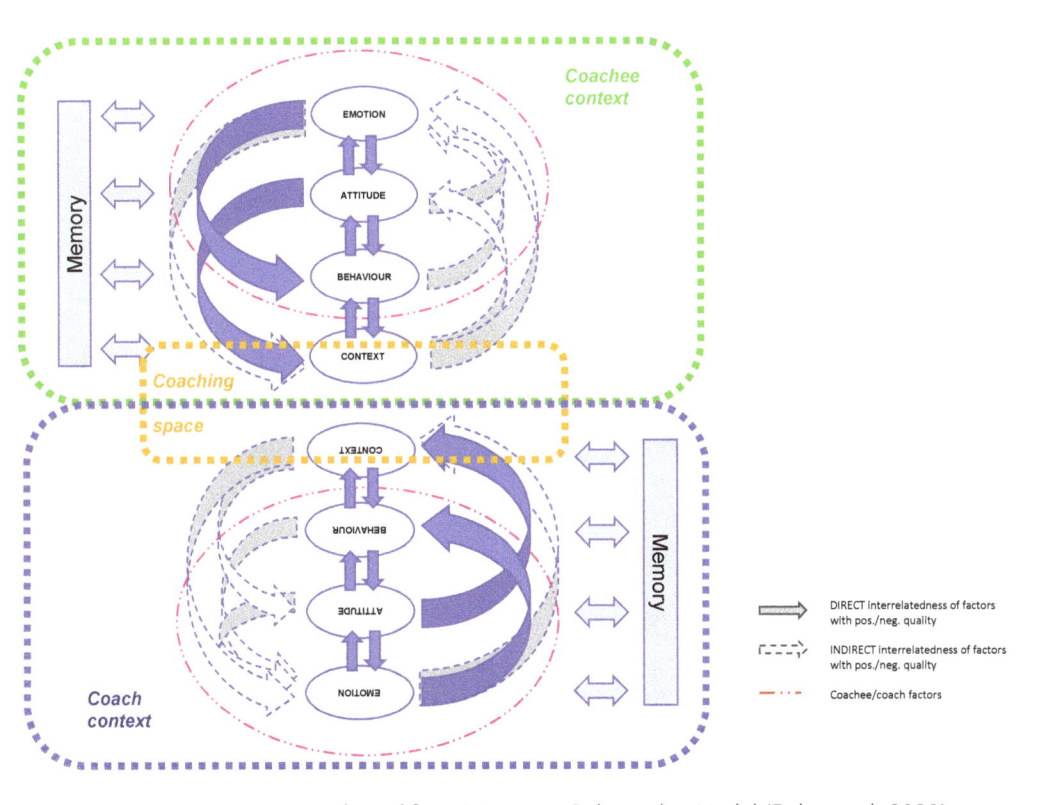

Adapted from Integrative Relationship Model (Erdös et al, 2020)

I think this evolution of the model helps underline the need for a coach, as the professional in the coaching relationship, to:

- ☐ Recognise the potential complexity in a coachee's challenge, and
- ☐ Be mindful of the many factors that may distort the coaching dialogue – not least what the coach themself brings to the relationship.
- ☐ Work to maintain the focus on the coachee's needs and interests and minimise the 'noise' in the relationship.

Coaching with 'I' – the coaching landscape

7.2 The outer context

The coaching relationship touches on a number of external contexts and influences affecting both coach and coachee:

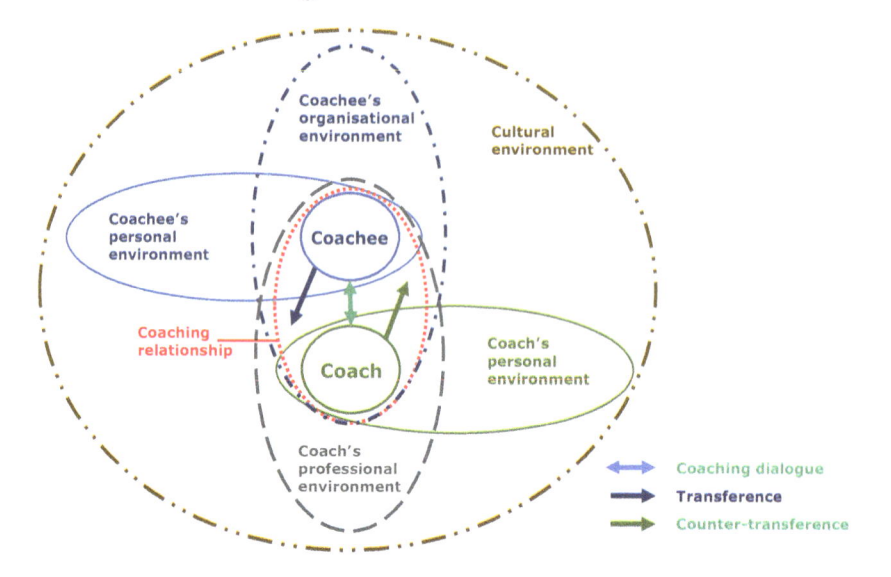

Environmental context for coaching

The influence and balance of all of these factors may need to be sorted through for the coachee to make progress. The diagram shows that multiple environments are in play in the coaching relationship. The balance and interaction of each of these environments – and how they affect a coachee – will tend to be unique to each coachee.

The complexity increases when corporate contracts frame the coaching relationship. For instance:

- ☐ Corporate clients will have their own views on the purpose of coaching and the objectives for each individual coachee. Corporate clients will also have a view on how they intend to assess the effectiveness of the coaching engagement. These views may or may not be founded on an understanding of how coaching works.

The coaching context

- The coach must look to defend their own commercial interests, whether they are operating on their own or as part of a company that provides coaching services. When a coach works through an intermediary, they may easily find that a 'simple' coaching engagement ends up with a set of contractual/relationship interactions a little like this:

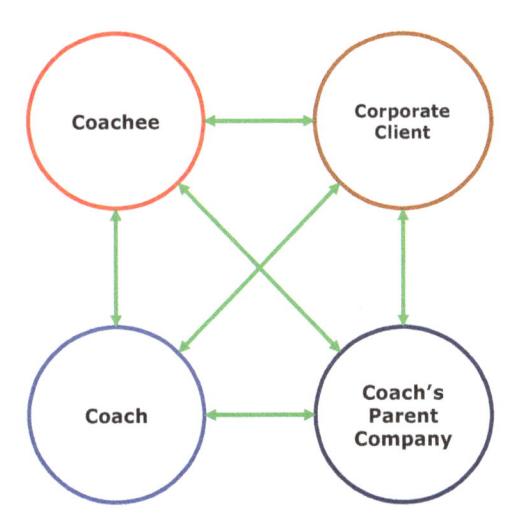

```
Coachee  <---->  Corporate Client
   ↑   ╲       ╱   ↑
   │    ╲    ╱     │
   ↓     ╲ ╱       ↓
Coach   <---->  Coach's Parent Company
```

This is clearly going to take some care to manage. In particular, the individual coaching relationship may risk being overshadowed by two sets of corporate expectations, which may or may not align with the needs of each individual coachee.

It follows that one key challenge for the coach may be to work through the range of external contexts with the individual coachee in order to build a relationship that is meaningful for both coachee and coach.

7.3 Keeping the focus on the coachee

One of the more common struggles for coaches (certainly for me over the years) is that we cannot escape our experience. Most coaches I know have done some other work first, so we bring to the coaching relationship a level of experience and understanding of many of the issues that a coachee faces. In effect, we are likely to have spent a considerable amount of time learning how to fix problems within our sphere of expertise. This is genuinely valuable experience, but, in the best interests of the coachee, we must overcome the urge (however pressing) to use that experience to 'fix our coachee'.

Each individual's experiences, outcomes, successes and failures are their own. We are not there to compel coachee thinking. Coaches may by all means let their experience inform their understanding of potential factors relevant to a coachee's situation. This may help them prompt the coachee to consider their situation fully and effectively. Coaches can, if the coachee asks, share their experiences. But, if they choose to do so, it is important that the coachee then analyses that experience *in their context* to decide what, if anything, they might turn to their use.

For coaches, learning to inform rather than advise their coachee also means that they must learn not to be disappointed if a coachee then chooses not to follow their coach's example.

7.4 Where does all that leave us?

- ☐ It is never just the coachee and the coach in a session – a cast of others is present (peers, employers/employees, friends etc.).
- ☐ Both coachee and coach bring to the work a complex understanding of the situation the coachee is focused on. They will not always be conscious of that understanding and may need to spend some time bringing their insight to the surface.
- ☐ In addition, where a corporate client is involved, there will probably be additional expectations, constraints and accountabilities which will need to be addressed.
- ☐ Where the coach is working through an intermediary (e.g. a coaching services company), that will tend to add to the complexity of the coaching engagement.

- Part of the work for the coachee is to understand where their challenge actually lies; and the things that they need to address to achieve a sustainable and resilient version of the change they seek.
- The onus is on the coach to maintain the focus on the coachee's needs and wants.

Part of the challenge of making a choice is understanding who is – and who should be – in charge of relevant patterns of behaviour.

Coaching with 'I' – the coaching landscape

Key takeaways

☐ The coaching relationship is rarely just about the coach and their coachee.

☐ There are inner contexts in play for both coachee and coach – mindsets driven by their experience and expectation.

☐ An Integrated Relationship Model is a handy way of mapping the inner contexts to help the coach and coachee identify and work them as required.

☐ External contexts are in play too, with potentially a range of stakeholders interested in the coaching relationship.

☐ Where coaching is commissioned through one or more corporate relationships, this adds further complexity to the relationship. It is for the coach to be aware of and manage any such issues.

☐ Coaches often come to the role with a wealth of relevant experience, but must resist the temptation to fix the coachee, based on their view. Coaches must ensure that the relationship enables the coachee to work with *their* challenges *in their context*.

8
Insights from the world of learning and development

At one level, it is obvious that learning and development must entail change. However, I've been involved in training, learning and development most of my professional life. It might surprise you to see how vigorously some people will resist the invitation to learn, to change, to develop – whatever the evidence of benefit. In fairness, part of the problem may be that, for many of us, our early experience of learning may have been less happy than we wanted. There is also a clear theme in western countries at least, that learning is something that is provided by – and only for – 'school' (which may stretch up to university).

Learning is actually a longer and more demanding journey than a few years at school; one that includes application over time (indeed over a lifetime). Learning should be about how someone moves from ignorance, through awareness, knowledge and skill to competence. Too often, however, that is not what people experience or pursue.

In the workplace, one of the key concerns is about value, about the combination of improvements in efficiency, effectiveness, productivity and profit. The balance of focus will differ between government, private enterprise and the third sector. All three sectors, however, are under relentless pressure to optimise performance. In such an environment, learning is going to be judged by its value – judged by the contribution of new thinking and new processes applied to make a difference to the workplace. In particular, in the current market, organisations will tend, rightly, to place a premium on:

- Insight – new, deeper, richer understanding of the business, the market, associated processes, risks and opportunities that then helps organisations improve performance.
- Innovation – cross-fertilising experience and insight from one context into another to create new opportunities to improve performance.
- Invention – conjuring up genuinely new offerings for the market that create a step change for the organisation.

One of the challenges for all of us in learning is recognising what we do and do not know; what we do and do not need to learn. We must begin by acknowledging that we have a performance gap in order to begin to progress. This awareness enables us to start to work through the competence development cycle:

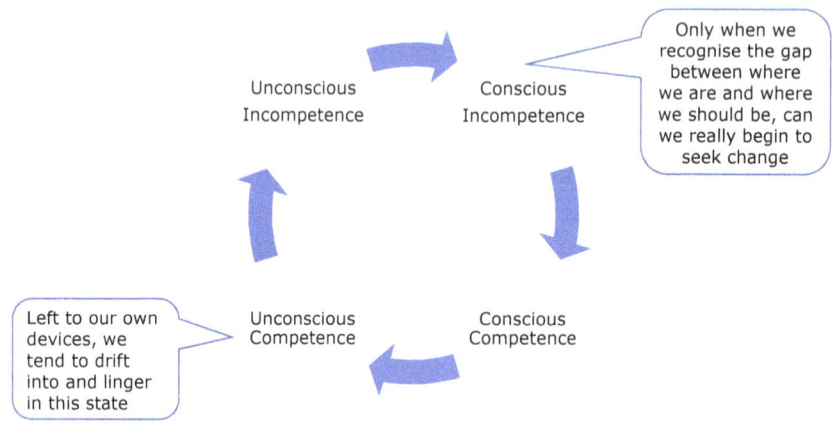

Competence development cycle (adapted from Broadwell, 1969)

The competence cycle can read a little starkly. Sometimes the performance challenge is indeed that the individual is missing knowledge/competence. As often, however, the coachee need is about recognising a gap between where they are and a worthwhile opportunity to perform better.

When a coachee comes to coaching, their awareness of their competence and any shortfall may be perfect. It is often not. Some may well understand where they are and come to coaching ready to work. Others might have only a partial understanding about gaps they need to address. Some will flat out fail to recognise that any improvement is worthwhile. There will also be a percentage who are unconscious of their true competence – that group tends to underestimate their capability and value. Finally, of course, some coachees will have been directed to a coach for 'remedial support'. Understandably, their starting point may be one of mistrust and resistance. For a range of reasons, therefore, coachees may need time to see – and value – opportunities for growth.

The coaching environment can be a safe place for coachees to reach an accurate understanding of their capabilities. They will, however, only be motivated and commit to development in those competence areas where they:

- ☐ Do feel safe (i.e. there is a mature tolerance of uncertainty, failure etc.)
- ☐ Acknowledge a gap that needs to be addressed
- ☐ Can see a tangible personal benefit to be gained.

8.1 Learning and learning styles

The journey to competence is rarely achieved in one mighty bound. Embedding learning requires thought, action and reflection. To make a real change, everyone needs to be ready to invest effort over time. Moreover, if becoming better takes time, then everyone needs to be motivated and to see some beneficial outcomes along the way, as well as in the end. Otherwise, they are more likely to lose heart and give up.

Emotion also plays into the process. Learning begins with recognising a gap – many people tend to internalise this as acknowledging a weakness. Learning also requires the student to flex their memory. As we know from the first section of this book, memory is suffused with emotion. In particular an emotion-laden memory, such as unhappy school days, can interfere with learning for a lot of people. The combined factors in play for learning look something like this:

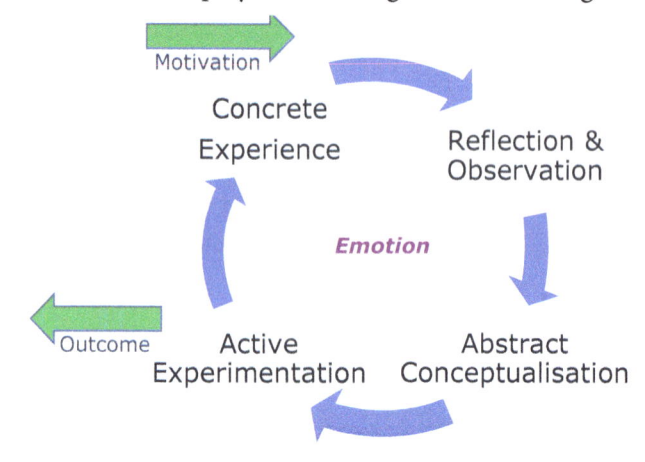

Learning cycle adapted from Kolb (1984)

In the workplace context, outcomes need to satisfy the employee and the organisation (which may sometimes mean the employee's line management, the responsible person in HR and someone in Finance). If a learning and development plan doesn't satisfy all of those stakeholders, it will tend to struggle for support in the organisation as a whole.

In the UK, commitment to employee training has been variable over much of the last 80 years (i.e. the post-world-war period). Organisations will commit to training required for legal compliance (e.g. health and safety, or professional body regulations). Beyond that, however, attitudes can vary between sectors and between organisations in a sector. They can even vary within organisations, especially where different divisions are competing with each other.

Those of us coaching in the UK would do well to remember that executive/business coaching is time-intensive, looks relatively expensive upfront and may not be welcomed by some stakeholders or the 'culture-in-practice' of an organisation we are working with.

Insights from the world of learning and development

If organisations commit to the idea but not the practice of learning and development, most staff will read the dissonance as lack of commitment – and respond accordingly. In those circumstances, learning doesn't happen.

There is a further dimension to the learner's experience. Research (e.g. Honey and Mumford, 2006) has shown that everyone tends to have a preferred learning style. This may be to play with an idea in their heads ('Theorist'), test it out with friends ('Pragmatist'), get out there and learn by doing ('Activist'), or model the new idea, review performance data and adjust ('Reflector').

There are several tests out there (e.g. the 4MAT Learning Style test) that can help someone work out their preferences. Most people prefer one or perhaps two styles and naturally tend to focus on those preferences – and avoid the others. However, note that each of those learning styles maps reasonably well to a stage of the learning cycle (see below). A person's learning styles may encourage them to stay in the area of the learning cycle that feels most comfortable. They then tend not to complete the learning cycle and so the learning is likely to fail to stick.

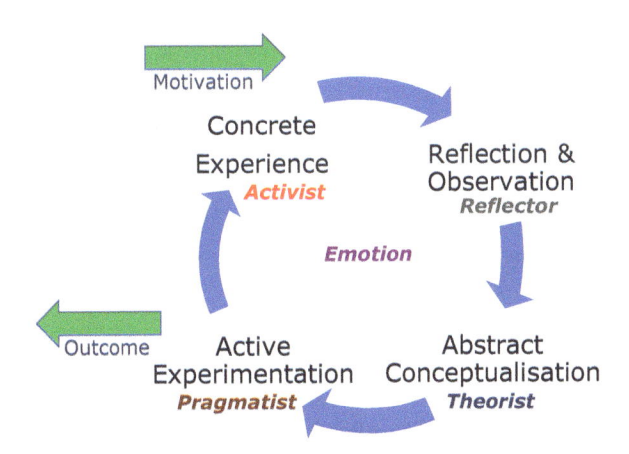

Mapping of learning cycle and learning styles, adapted from Kolb (1984) and Honey and Mumford (2006)

We should also consider the neuro-linguistic programming (NLP) take on this. NLP suggests that our brains have a preference for either Visual, Auditory, Kinaesthetic, Olfactory or Gustatory processing of information. The 'VAKOG' mapping is sometimes modelled as a learning style. In my experience, it can be a handy way of choosing the practices we adopt in learning. It does not, however, offer a quick pass around the legwork implied in the Kolb/Honey and Mumford cycle.

8.2 Conditions for effective learning

It is a truth universally acknowledged that education/learning is a key factor in individual social mobility and economic well-being; and in societal democratisation, growth and stability. Yet, gaining a basic grounding to live and work in today's societies, never mind being able to pursue lifelong education and learning, is still at best an aspiration in so many countries. In some of the more troubled places of the world, this is because governments actively stand against education – for the simple reason that its potential benefits threaten their control and interests. But, even in more democratic or liberal countries, the practical commitment to education/learning may be muted. In part, this reflects patterns of thinking that frame education and learning as belonging to our schooldays, not about 'real life'. This also reflects a tendency to assume that learning is a simple process.

I hope I've shown already that there is much more to the learning process – not least the practical constraint that we can only develop competence over time. But the conditions for learning matter too. In particular, the following factors can strongly influence how effectively we learn:

    ☐ *Recognition* – each individual needs to recognise the opportunity/need. This is obvious at 'school' (a place of learning), but people tend to shy away from recognition in adulthood. We all need to do better as adults and managers at fairly and constructively identifying and agreeing ongoing learning effort. We also need to acknowledge that it is not to be reserved just for addressing incompetence, it's about all of us adding value through improved performance (good to great, great to class leading etc.).

- ☐ *Engagement* – learning takes time and effort and involves a process beyond just reading/observation/being told. If we don't engage properly with the whole learning cycle, we won't really progress – it's as simple as that.

- ☐ *Belief* – mindset is fundamental to learning. A growth mindset embraces change and learning. Fixed mindsets struggle to believe it's worth the effort and may (subconsciously) resist. More specifically, each individual needs to believe that they *can* learn and that their learning will be worthwhile.

- ☐ *Undertaking* – recognition, engagement and belief all matter. But we also have to put in the effort for as long as it takes to achieve results. That may mean changing our daily schedule to make time to study, practise and reflect. Recalling what we have seen about learning preferences and the learning cycle, undertaking may also mean changing/extending our learning habits and practices to ensure that our learning is fully embedded.

- ☐ *Support* – the right support can make a big difference: most of us can point to a teacher who directly affected our attitude to a subject. Such influences continue to matter later on in life, too, as progress is rarely a solo performance. Thus, especially for major learning activities, we should be clear about and ensure we have the support we need to help us manage, study, practise and sometimes just plain vent our frustrations about our learning journey. One person might be able to do all that for us (assuming of course they can devote themselves entirely to our needs!). For the majority of us, however, this will mean having several people in our support network.

Coaching with 'I' – the coaching landscape

All five factors ('REBUS') tilting in the right direction make a big difference to an individual's willingness to learn and their ability to do so efficiently and effectively. And adult learning does matter. For those that need a visual stimulus to help make the point about conditions for the learning journey, here's a rebus for REBUS:

Bus image from pixabay

There is a basic logic here. All around us, the pace of change has increased and many of the accelerating trends in work and life are not well understood by most of us. In particular, the rate of change of information-based solutions and applications is bewildering. In some respects, it is creating a fight, flight or freeze response: we try to do it all, becoming lost in the process, or we simply step back and hope it won't harm our career prospects. Neither response seems likely to serve us well.

If we accept that we need to act more constructively, then we have to:

- ☐ Understand what skills we need
- ☐ Work out the right level of competence we need in order to be effective in our organisation/sector
- ☐ Work out the effort we need to put into refreshing/maintaining our skills
- ☐ Monitor for new skills that we may need to learn in order to stay on top of our game
- ☐ Have an agreed and funded learning plan and support in place.

All of this would seem to call for a different, perhaps more systematic approach to our adult learning. It also implies a different relationship with employers, which would reshape our approach to working time and practical commitment to learning etc.

To bring this back into the coaching landscape, as coaches, we can help coachees build and sustain their conditions for learning. The coaching dialogue often identifies opportunities/needs for learning (supporting Recognition) and provides an effective space for helping coachees see the value of engaging and believing in learning for their benefit (Engagement).

For many who find the challenge difficult, one particularly strong blocker is a negative/fixed mindset. I notice a lot of this in respect of arithmetic/corporate financials or public speaking. We can help coachees reconfigure their mindset and build a learning path they can manage (Belief). In terms of action, we may sometimes help by being directly involved in training, mentoring or helping coachees identify suitable sources of training/mentoring (Undertaking). Beyond that, I think most coaches would be familiar with being part of a coachee's support mechanism when they are learning (Support).

8.3 The coach's role supporting learning and development

As coaches, our primary role is not training/instruction. That said, if we are to help our coachees understand the opportunities before them, then we need at least to understand something of the learning process and the potential pitfalls for our coachee. We also need to understand how to encourage the coachee to commit fully to the learning cycle. This has a number of implications for the coach.

8.3.1 Meta-competence

The coach may not be training as such, but it helps to understand the basic learning mechanisms and potential challenges for their coachees.

This means that competence in assessing and managing the competence development process matters. In that sense, the coach must work in a space of 'conscious meta-competence':

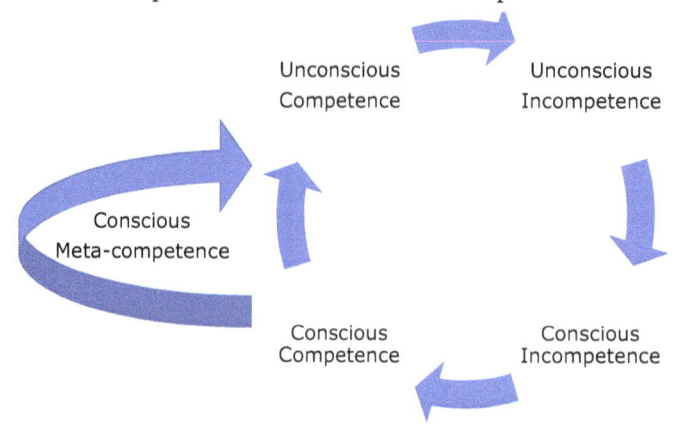

Competence development, adapted from Broadwell (1969)

8.3.2 It begins with Recognition

The first hurdle to overcome is for the coachee to recognise the opportunity or need. As we have seen, the coachee's starting point can be in several places. We often find that coachees have become trapped in 'bubblethink' (i.e. locked in their own framing pattern) about their knowledge and their capacity/capability to learn. Self-doubt, criticism from others, blind spots and so on can all contribute to coachees having a closed mind when it comes to the question of learning. As a consequence, a coach's (initial) contribution may be to provide some 'outsight' – an independent, external perspective on the coachee's thinking to help them re-think the possibility of learning and developing.

A common stumbling block in this space is a belief that some skills, such as leadership, are innate. This can block both Recognition (they can't see the opportunity to learn) and the Belief that they can do it anyway. However:

- ☐ If something is a skill, that means there are tools, techniques and processes involved – these can all be learned.

Insights from the world of learning and development

- In the workplace, coachees may simply be falling victim to magical thinking. As part of imagining their goal, they tend to conjure an image of someone who is competent; and, usually, they have not seen this exemplar developing their skill. Coachees may then fall into the trap of concluding that their model simply has that ability, which must somehow be 'natural', like magic(!). But it would serve them better to recognise that their benchmark individual was once where they are now – that their journey is therefore possible too.

8.3.3 Helping the coachee understand their learning style

In general, when people think about their learning style, they tend to focus simply on the tools they used to get through our exams. As coaches, we can help our coachees better understand their learning strengths and potential weaknesses.

Recall the Kolb/Honey and Mumford cycle:

Motivation

Concrete Experience
Activist

Reflection & Observation
Reflector

Emotion

Outcome Active Experimentation
Pragmatist

Abstract Conceptualisation
Theorist

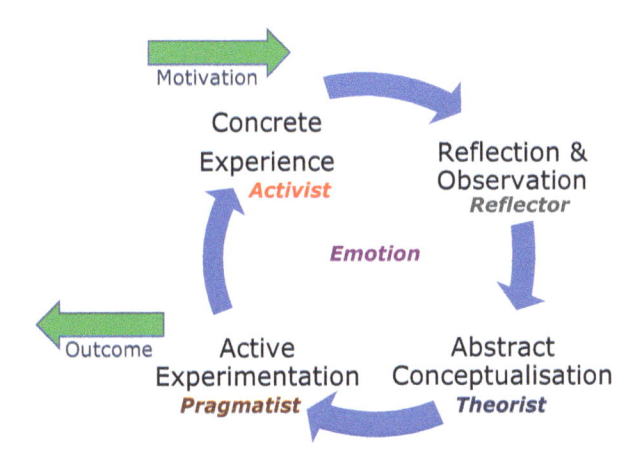

Mapping of learning cycle and learning styles, adapted from Kolb (1984) and Honey and Mumford (2006)

As discussed (chapter 8.1), there are several tools to help coaches do this. In practice, coachees tend to recognise their preferred style(s)

103

readily. They may find it harder to see the value of the other styles – it may be useful to analyse a simple worked example (relevant to something they care about) to demonstrate the point.

8.3.4 Helping the coachee commit to the full learning cycle

At the very least, as coaches we should check the coachee's knowledge of the learning cycle and help them understand the value of completing the cycle to maximise learning achievement and impact. We might usefully test their learning plan to see whether a full cycle of learning activities is included. With my coachees, we not only discuss their plan, but review progress – first, because it is helpful in itself for the specific learning topic; second because it reinforces the more general learning habit of think, do, review.

8.3.5 Helping the coach manage their learning

There are clearly some implications for coaches in all this:

- ☐ There's a lot to learn.
- ☐ The coach's learning takes time too, so they need to think about and plan how they will manage it.
- ☐ There needs to be a balance between focusing on a given tool/technique and the relationship with the coachee. For me, the relationship with the coachee always takes priority, even if that sometimes means living with a technical mistake with a tool/exercise etc.

Key takeaways

- ☐ The coachee's journey is a learning journey. An understanding of the relevant aspects of learning theory will strengthen the support coaches provide.

- ☐ The learning arc tracks from ignorance to competence. It is competence that delivers value for the individual and their organisation.

- ☐ The Learning Cycle and Learning Styles models underline the importance of thinking, trialling, doing and reflection in order to embed learning well.

- ☐ The conditions for effective learning also matter: Recognition, Engagement, Belief, Undertaking and Support. The coach can help their coachee build and sustain the right conditions.

- ☐ The coach is facilitator in this process and part of their role is to help their coachee through the end-to-end journey to their desired competence level.

9
The core coaching intentions: expose, explore, evolve

Coaches, especially as new coaches, can find themselves presented with a bewildering array of tools and techniques. There seems to be an army of real and virtual salespeople out to persuade them to invest in the latest silver bullet solution for our coachees. This can all feel quite daunting and not a little confusing. From my experience, and that of many of my peers, it seems helpful to recognise early on that:

- ☐ There is no silver bullet. You know it, your coachee knows it. In the face of difficult challenges, reaching for a silver bullet could look like an appealing option. It isn't. More often than not, silver bullet thinking is little more than a short route to disappointment and frustration.

- ☐ As a general rule, the tool is much less important than the use we and our coachees make of it. With that in mind, our intention is probably a more useful guide for how we build our coaching skills.

9.1 Expose, explore and evolve

For me, there are three core coaching intentions that frame the work that we do: expose, explore and evolve.

9.1.1 Expose

The real nature of the challenges or goals on the coachee's mind needs to be held fully in the light. The coachee's challenge or goal is often not what they initially thought it was. This seems to be particularly common in cases where there is a conflict between what the coachee really wants and what they think is expected of them (by e.g. their managers, their organisation or their sector). The coachee may not be fully aware of their true aspiration, so it can take them time to get there.

Some coachees actively suppress what they really want. This suppression may be unconscious, borne out of a habit of risk avoidance or imposter syndrome etc. But it may be a conscious act too. Coachees in highly competitive cultures may be concerned about admitting to a perceived weakness, especially if they doubt the confidentiality of the coaching relationship. Similarly, coachees ordered to take coaching as a remedial intervention may suspect the coach's (and their employer's) intentions. These undercurrents need to be brought to the surface and dealt with for the coachee to be able to move on with confidence. There may, therefore, need to be several rounds of expose dialogue during the coaching engagement (indeed even within a single session) as a coachee discovers the true boundaries of their concerns.

Where a corporate client is in play, their perspective and narrative may be completely different from that of our coachee. On top of that, the coachee may not be aware of the corporate narrative. As a result, the coachee may also need some time to work through the implications of the corporate client's perspective for their individual choices.

9.1.2 Explore

As we saw in the first part of this book, so much of what goes on in the brain/mind is interconnected in complex ways. This means that there is usually a fair chance that the coachee's challenge or goal, as presented, is only the tip of the iceberg. If they are looking to make a real, sustainable change, they will need to understand enough of their challenge/goal's complexity to be able to shift the balance. In essence, you rarely make a great race horse by improving just the one leg.

I have also found explore activity to be particularly helpful in shifting a coachee's attention away from recognising the problem and towards discovering potential solutions. A challenge/problem that has been brewing for a while can seem larger and more impenetrable than it really is. Explore activity helps map the coachee's landscape, put their challenge into perspective and define the things they want to deal with in more manageable terms.

Clearly, there is likely to be some interplay between expose and explore activity. Exposing one concern can lead to an unexpected exploration of a number of ideas/experiences. Equally, exploration can unexpectedly highlight a challenge that the coachee wants to be brought to light. As coaches, we need to follow the appropriate flow of a session. By recapping what has been explored, what has been exposed and what should be attended to next, however, we can help our coachees make the right call for themselves between potential areas for focus.

9.1.3 Evolve

Learning and development is about change. Sometimes this can be quite dramatic – the lightning strikes and we finally see how to do things in a better way. More often, change is about practice, persistence and time. So, if the coachee is not committed to change, it will not happen. Some coachees, while eager to change, will need to acquire new skills, or apply existing skills in a new way in order to build a realistic vision of:

- ☐ What they want
- ☐ What good looks like
- ☐ How they get there

- ☐ The support network they need and
- ☐ How they will sustain motivation from start to finish.

The 'REBUS' learning conditions checklist (chapter 8.2) can help coachees work out what they need.

For evolution to be meaningful to our coachees (and potentially other stakeholders in their effort), there needs to be some form of proof. This helps consolidate and celebrate their progress. It also helps coachees sustain their efforts. Any evolve activity therefore needs to include agreeing on tracking evidence/measures of change.

9.1.4 Working with expose, explore, evolve

It's worth noting that expose and explore activity can be challenging for some coachees. Both require acknowledging a need to change and/or acknowledging a shortfall. Both may involve dealing with boundaries around ethics, personal behaviour, or some of a coachee's less favourable personality traits, Because of the potential complexity involved, it may take a little time for the coachee to be willing to embrace the process wholeheartedly. Coachees may need continuing support to get there. Without that commitment, they are more likely not to put in the work to evolve.

We should also be clear that there is a boundary for the coach to manage in all of this. The relationship we are looking at here is coaching – not counselling, nor therapy. Expose, explore and evolve activity will bring to the surface a range of issues affecting coachee performance and therefore be of interest in the coaching context. Some of those issues may lie outside the coach's formal competence – they may be better suited to counselling or therapy for example. It is the coach's responsibility to manage that boundary effectively, both for their own and the coachee's sake. The coach may therefore need to encourage their coachee to seek support elsewhere. By implication, as coaches, we should have some idea of what other professional support may be readily available to the coachee.

Coaching with 'I' – the coaching landscape

If the challenge of expose and explore is about confronting the whole self, then the challenge of evolve is about sustaining effort and momentum. As a consequence, the coaching dialogue is likely to be have emphasis on motivation, recalling and engaging the coachee support network and revisiting the targeted goals and benefits. In practice, this is likely to happen several times in an extended period of coachee development.

The expose, explore, evolve intentions may seem to imply a linear journey. Some of the work with coachees will be like that, but with the big challenges, there may in practice be a much more fluid movement between the relevant activities. Coachee clarity on their focus can really help them analyse their challenge/goal effectively and so speed up their process. In practice, I have found it helpful to try to be explicit about which intention the coachee is focused on. I find this helps them into a way of thinking and rethinking their challenge or goal.

9.1.5 Articulating the change journey

One of the challenges a coachee faces in developing a new skill and competence can be to articulate their effort, process and progress effectively. They have to learn the language of their skill as part of building their skill and competence. We have to help our coachees do that too.

The following comments apply to developing any new competence. They take on a particularly interesting flavour when the coaching work is focused on the development of competence in the so-called soft skills. This is a common focus of senior/executive coaching, so keep that in mind as we go through the rest of this section.

Business theory has been clear for some considerable time about the importance of soft skills to the effective functioning of an organisation (and in particular to the career prospects of those who would lead). Despite this, training and understanding in those skills continues to lag behind. As a consequence, coachees may struggle to articulate their needs and progress with soft skills. That can easily become a barrier to putting in the effort to improve.

How then, do we help coachees develop their ability to articulate their soft skills journey? There are 3 'languages' to think about: the coachee's personal language, their professional language and the coach's professional language.

9.1.5.1 The coachee's personal language

None of us would be comfortable being asked to describe our ability to speak a language in a language we don't yet speak. So, our coachees will need to find a frame and vocabulary to help them as they evolve their soft skills. In practice, I have found that the language of personality assessments can be helpful in building up confidence and competence in working with and talking about soft skills. These tools provide helpful terms to describe preferences/traits and how they affect behaviour. They also provide a framework for understanding our own disposition and how different personalities can communicate more effectively with each other. None of the tools out there is a complete answer, but most of them can be used as a solid stepping stone for coachees.

9.1.5.2 The coachee's professional language

We also need to embrace the coachee context here. The coachee's organisation, sector and/or profession will have their own language/terms about learning and development. The culture and people in these contexts will also have their way of talking about and practising soft skills. It can be very helpful for the coachee to couch their journey and insights in those corporate/sectoral/professional terms, as this will help them better:

- ☐ Understand and address their employer's (and sector etc.) expectations and needs.
- ☐ Be consistent with their organisation's cultural norms when dealing with peers and staff.
- ☐ Articulate their progress, insight, needs etc. to their corporate, professional and other stakeholders.

Coaching with 'I' – the coaching landscape

Clearly, where you have been engaged as a coach through a corporate client, you will need to respond to/work with client language too.

9.1.5.3 The coach's professional language

As coaches, we can spend a lot of time developing our competence and learning to apply particular tools and techniques. We will naturally tend to favour some models/tools more than others – and so to favour the language those models use. In many cases, however, the language of our approaches to – or tools for – coaching are not common to the workplace. So, in helping our coachees, we will often need to take time to teach the model to our coachees and/or translate our professional language into terms that work for them.

9.2 The importance of evidence

We saw in the first part of this book that the brain is a complex beast. It is brilliant and makes incredible use of a range of short-cuts (patterns and approximation in particular). But it is both fallible and vulnerable to distortion (not just in terms of accuracy, but through the influence of emotional attachments to our experiences and memories).

Further, when coachees seek to review and change, they often find themselves battling on several fronts:

- They may not understand how their brain/mind has been involved in causing the challenge they are now trying to address.
- The brain's short-cuts are generally effective – and efficient. Doing something different means putting in energy and effort. Nobody should be surprised, then, if the brain tries to resist the extra demand.
- Doing something different can also feel like accepting failure. Best case, this may be failure to see the need for change earlier. Worst case, they may be tempted to read their current situation as a failure in them – especially if they are already vulnerable to Imposter Syndrome/'I'm not good enough' thinking.

The core coaching intentions: expose, explore, evolve

- ☐ We all tend to take our patterns and recalled experience as shorthand for our sense of 'I'. So, deciding to change can in some sense feel like a direct challenge to 'I' for some. This can be both exhilarating and terrifying at times.
- ☐ Some coachees will be less familiar/comfortable with how to articulate all this.

As a consequence, as the coachee moves to change, they may actively resist the practical steps required. Moreover, their resistance may or may not be conscious.

For all of these reasons, it is really important to help the coachee build clear, solid evidence at each stage of their effort. In particular, evidence can help support the coachee as they accept that something isn't working for them; and as they accept the need for, then commit to change. They also need to see that the effort is worthwhile (or why bother?). Evidence of how things are changing can therefore help sustain a coachee through the process.

The evidence the coachee builds needs to be valid and indisputable – it does not have to be cheery all the time. As change progresses, things may get worse before they get better. Trying out a new skill or tool, for example, can feel very clunky for both the coachee and their colleagues as everyone tries to adjust to a different way of working and relating with each other. Provided a coachee understands the potential for dips in the road, then evidence of a dip corroborates the planned journey. If the coachee does not know what to expect, then negative evidence can be derailing. It is therefore important that a coachee can see their journey in a realistic context.

I hope it is clear, then, that coachees need to keep linking decisions and reviews to evidence. The metrics agreed as part of contracting can help with this (see Chapter 12). Certainly, if the coachee has clear line of sight from their planned action to an outcome of their coaching effort, they are more likely to be motivated. The line of sight does not have to be a single jump – after all that is rarely the case. It just has to be clearly visible to the coachee. Moreover, as coaches, we may need to help the coachee identify additional tactical milestones/evidence as they take each action.

9.3 Tools to support expose, explore, evolve

So what tools might we use? There is tremendous choice out there – and no end of salespeople trying to sell us the latest 'must have' tool for our coaching practice. For new coaches in particular, this can all feel rather bewildering. For building my own toolkit, I am generally guided by:

- ☐ Determining how well a tool/technique supports expose, explore and evolve intentions. More often than not, the better tools can be used effectively with two or three of the intentions.

- ☐ Having a range of tools to apply to different learning styles – and so resonate more readily with a particular coachee.

- ☐ Identifying tools/techniques that relate to specific issues we are likely to encounter in coaching (see common challenges section later). Common topics for such tools include emotional intelligence or values. I will then spend time working out how the use of the tool might alter in the different operations or with different learning styles to help me land it effectively with a coachee.

- ☐ Preferring tools/techniques that generate evidence to support the coachee's thinking and action.

This framework helps me to focus on tools/techniques that will be useful; and to cast a more analytical eye on new tools/techniques offered up to the profession.

Key takeaways

- There are three core intentions for coaching: expose, explore, evolve.
    - Expose seeks to get at the coachee's real concern.
    - Explore maps the coachee's landscape.
    - Evolve focuses on supporting the coachee's change journey.
- Personality assessment tools can provide a useful framing language to help coachees talk about their development journey with soft skills.
- Clear and compelling evidence is a key underpinning for the coaching dialogue. It can help the coachee identify areas for change; and sustain them as they put options into action.
- Faced with the vast range of tools available, select tools that:
    - Meet your practice needs
    - Apply to a range of learning styles, to increase the chances of tools working with different coachees.

10
Models for talking about the mind

If a coachee is going to understand the work needed to make change happen, it can really help them to understand better what's going on inside their brain/mind. This is in keeping with the principles of Broadwell's model – knowing that we do not know (conscious incompetence) is the real start of the learning journey. As coaches, I believe it is worth our having to hand some ways to help the coachee get to grips with what's going on.

Although some of the basic ideas about brain and mind and 'I' are relatively simple to start off with, things become complicated quite quickly. Start to delve into the detail of the relevant psychology and neuroscience and, inevitably, there is much jargon and (albeit for good reasons) the material can be fairly impenetrable. Nonetheless, for those coaches and coachees who relish such a challenge, head to the Internet, get started and the best of luck! For those who want to get to grips with the basic ideas, I hope this book will be a starter and encourage you to research further.

For most coachees, it is helpful to have an effective model to set out and explore the key ideas. There is value for the majority of people in being able to visualise a process. For some, the cognitive cycle I've used in this book will work well enough, but, as we have seen, stories are compelling and easier to remember. I have therefore summarised below my take[2] on two of the more popular stories about how the brain seems to work.

---

[2] And to that extent, while I've tried to represent the models accurately, any errors will be mine.

Models for talking about the mind

The first thing to point out is that they are models, so there is an element of sacrificing accuracy and detail for the sake of something that is comprehensible and usable. They are not an exact description of what is going on. Rather, they both offer a concise and coherent way to articulate what is happening in our brains – and to help everyone (plan to) do things differently.

I recognise that there is a large variety of models to consider. I have chosen these two because:

- They are established and clear models that capture the key points effectively.
- They make sense to a lot of people – and are relatively easy to explain. I have certainly found that coachees tend to adopt these models readily.
- Each model has a slightly different emphasis in its language – one resonates more with those who think in terms of systems, the other with those who think in terms of relationships. So, together, they are likely to appeal to quite a broad audience.
- There is a lot of published material about both models, which means that both coaches and coachees can easily learn more and make better use of their preferred model.

As you read through the two descriptions, I expect that you will naturally prefer one of them. It doesn't matter which and if either is helpful then that is to the good. The key point here is that a coachee's needs take precedence. As coaches, we need to be ready to work with whichever model best resonates with a coachee and best helps them get to grips with the relevant ideas. On that basis, I recommend spending some time becoming familiar with both models, the original works and the detail they offer in order to support your client/coachee engagement properly.

Coaching with 'I' – the coaching landscape

10.1 System I, System II Thinking

Daniel Kahneman is primarily associated with this model through his work *Thinking, Fast and Slow*. The basic premise is that two systems drive brain activity:

System I – Fast

This system has the following main characteristics:

- ☐ It is automatic.
- ☐ It is effortless.
- ☐ It is generally unconscious and without self-awareness.
- ☐ It is not about control, even if the consequence of some of its activity is to determine (and so 'control') what we think, say and do.
- ☐ It assesses the situation and provides updates.

System II – Slow

This system has the following main characteristics:

- ☐ It is deliberate.
- ☐ It is effortful.
- ☐ It is conscious and self-aware.
- ☐ This system is about control.
- ☐ It calls for data and makes decisions.

System I is responsible for 98% of our decision making. System II is then responsible for the remaining 2%. So, just to reinforce this point: c.98% of our decision-making is automatic, generally unconscious and not self-aware.

System I uses heuristics (remember: short-cuts, such as patterns and approximation) to develop and apply practical solutions that are good enough. That 'good enough' perspective helps the system run fast. In the context of our discussion in section 1 of this book, System I tends to be the 'home' of the patterns we use.

System II is more about deliberate focus. It deals with the difficult thinking and, as a result, tends to take more time deciding on a course of action. System II thinking also requires deliberate effort. One weakness of System II is that, because of its active focus, it can create one or more blind spots to any activity not immediately in its sights.

In part because of its speed, System I is dominant and drives System II activity. System II can intervene, however, and change the decision being made.

10.1.1 System I – System II and making a choice

In this model, making a choice will mean activating System II – so we need to think about some ways we can do that. We need to achieve two things:

- Hitting the brakes on System I behaviour to give us the thinking time we need. Typically, the practice is to build a catalogue of warning markers. So, let's take the example of giving up smoking. If we know that we tend to scramble for a cigarette after a team meeting, we can start to create a routine (not involving smoking) for the end of meetings which delays our action and helps System II to step in and resist the temptation.

- Improving System II engagement and processes will help us to assert more control over our decision making. When we know what behaviours we want to change or develop, we can start to build a script that complies with the new behaviour. Some of my coachees have even written out their script and posted it somewhere relevant in order to help them with this. The script or mini-plan helps keep System II in charge (because it makes the new action easier and less resource-intensive). Over time, of course, the brain will adopt the new script as a pattern to store in System I.

From what we have said here, you might also conclude that learning needs to engage both System I and System II in order to establish effective and efficient behaviours. In particular, coachees can find it helpful to put new scripts in place around the phases/types of learning activity they tend to find harder. These scripts can be used to create clusters of associations (as images, or stories etc.), so that the associations form part of the pattern that System I adopts. This then helps improve recall of blocks of information rather than just single items.

10.2 The Chimp Paradox

This model was developed by Steve Peters and reflects thinking developed to stunning effect in the context of sports coaching. Professor Peters and Chimp Management Ltd continue to develop the thinking. There are three core elements to the model:

- ☐ The Computer

  The Computer manages the brain's storage and automatic processes and works across the brain. In our context, it runs the brain's programmes (patterns!) and will keep doing that until it hits a snag. It will then raise the alarm with the rest of the brain.

- ☐ The Human
  This element is associated with the brain's frontal lobe, this is the manifestation of our mature, rational thought and judgement (sounds a bit like System II). For our purposes, this is the conscious 'I' stepping into action.

- ☐ The Chimp
  The third main element in the model is the Chimp, which is associated with the limbic system in the brain and our emotional processes. In that sense, it is the manifestation of subconscious – instinct, emotion, our primal needs.

Models for talking about the mind

In our day-to-day, the Computer is in charge – our patterns and short-cuts happily taking us through our regular tasks. When there is something unexpected, or there appears to be a problem, the Computer raises the alarm. Both the Human and the Chimp then attempt to respond. The Computer needs instruction, so waits for the other two to get their act together. The Chimp is generally bigger, stronger and faster than the Human – so usually gets there first. Hence, our reactions under pressure are likely to be more about instinct and primal need than conscious, considered thought.

This all takes some moments to explain, but remember, this sequence plays out in our brains at the brain's operating speed (see chapter 1.1). Thus, the gap between alarm and solution may barely be noticeable, especially if the Chimp wins the race. If we want to put the Human in charge, we're going to have to work at it.

This model also recognises the potential for glitches/gremlins to get into the workings of the Computer and so distort perception, interpretation and choice of action. This sounds rather like the errors in our patterns that we discussed earlier. The point about glitches is that we tend not to know they're there. As a consequence, the Computer will plough on regardless, while the Chimp and the Human may notice nothing, or perhaps, at some level, a gut feeling that something is amiss.

In this model, the Computer has no interest in change, the Chimp will be wary of it. Both, however, need to be managed if the Human is to drive learning, change etc.

10.2.1 The Chimp Paradox and making a choice

The strategy story is slightly different with the Chimp Paradox. There are two types of challenge to think about:

- ☐ A known problem. When the Computer hits a problem, it sends out an error code, seeking help. The challenge now is to delay the Chimp to allow the Human to take charge. So, the trick is to calm or distract the Chimp. Again, where there are circumstances we know may cause a problem, we can start to prepare scripts to help the Human take control.

- ☐ An unknown problem (glitches). As none of the actors in the Chimp story know there's an issue, more work is going to be involved. First the glitch has to be identified. Only then can we develop a plan to deal with the Computer, delay the Chimp (who will be suspicious of any attempt to change how things are) and let the Human guide the new action.

In both the Two System and Chimp models, there is a notion of existing patterns (the heuristic activity, or the computer's programmes) that are for some reason unhelpful. Learning and development activity implies that at least some patterns may have to be unlearned and or replaced by new patterns. Both models can help frame that discussion. The Chimp model is more explicit than System I about the fact that change needs to address the practical (the Computer) as well as the emotional (the Chimp).

Most coachees I have worked with have responded positively to one model or the other. Both have proved an effective starting point. For those thinking about being coached, the models can also provide a handy doorway into discussion about apparent inconsistencies or contradictions in someone's patterns of choice.

Key takeaways

- ☐ Once they start working on how their mind/brain works, most coachees find it helpful to have a model as a reference point.

- ☐ System I – System II Thinking offers a systemic view of the core reaction process. It identifies the key functions of each System – pointing us to the work we need to do to make changes.

- ☐ The Chimp Paradox offers a more relational model, showing how three core mind/brain elements (Computer, Human and Chimp) work/fight together. This helps us start managing the behaviours and relationships in order to make changes.

- ☐ A good model is one that is effective for the coachee. This means that, as coaches, we need to be comfortable with a range of models to increase the chances of being able to find a good match for each of our coachees.

11
Coaching focus

One practical challenge for the coach will often be to deal with the differences (not to say contradictions) between:

- Corporate client focus – typically about encouraging conformance with corporate cultural expectations and aspirations, and

- Coachee focus – they are naturally more concerned with their own development (so may be more thinking about their own way).

Sorting out which concerns are in play (and dominant) before entering into a contract can save a lot of confusion later on.

11.1 Corporate client focus

Corporate clients come to coaching with a variety of goals in mind. Where organisations are leading, they may look to external coaching to:

- Improve organisational performance, where coaching is just another tool in learning and development (L&D) strategy.

- Act as a positive incentive/reward for staff. The idea is that the company is investing in the individual as a marker of trust and acknowledgement.

- Stir up the mindset at different levels of leadership within the organisation. The idea here is to give leaders the opportunity to re-think and possibly redirect.

- Drive cultural change by helping key individuals rethink and refocus the organisation.

☐ Act as a remedial intervention. Here, coaching can be used to tackle weak or inappropriate performance. From the coach's perspective, this is the least desirable, because it sets the individual coachee in a negative context before you've even started. That, in turn, can set trust and rapport back a step or two.

11.1.1 Changing workplace dynamics and corporate client focus on culture change

One particular aspect of organisational culture may be worth drawing out here. For much of the 20th century, production (the factory) and productivity (ergonomics) tended to dominate business thinking across the West. The focus was on larger scale operations with a high degree of task specialisation. This led to individual work roles being carefully defined and constrained. Employees were typically expected to master a very limited set of skills, then apply them efficiently and with minimum thinking. In other words, unconscious competence was often set as the ideal outcome within the workplace.

As we moved towards the end of the 20th century, things became more complicated. Business operations and employee roles became increasingly complex. More and more employees were expected to have an awareness of what was going on, to analyse their task and then adapt. Such a behavioural set requires a conscious competence and requires staff to be operating with conscious competence for much more of their time.

Leaders and managers, meanwhile, are now expected to bring a broader understanding of their role – with individual expertise, operating context knowledge, innovation, sector knowledge, market knowledge, broader socio-political understanding etc. – to bear on their work. It is becoming common to expect leaders and managers to understand how to drive change, innovation and even invention successfully; and to do so while maintaining current productivity.

Coaching with 'I' – the coaching landscape

At every level, there seems to be a shift towards more complex, more conscious performance, which, if done well:

- ☐ Makes organisations more efficient/profitable
- ☐ Enriches individual work
- ☐ Promotes a more innovative and collaborative mindset throughout the organisation's culture.

But getting there can mean rethinking work across the entire organisation.

A workplace that values unconscious competence tends to work on rules, processes and compliance. That tends not to involve much conversation. A workplace that moves to operating more as a *conscious collective,* needs interactive reflection, exploration and analysis at every level: it needs to be a place of conscious competence (and conscious meta-competence). Managing the corporate conversation in this scenario becomes a critical task/competence, which, when achieved, tends to encourage a more mobile organisational culture – and structure. Given that coaching works in the space of reflection, exploration and analysis, it is a natural tool to help people rethink. Hence, corporate clients have increasingly come to turn to coaching to help drive cultural change.

11.2 Coachee focus

There are multiple aims at the individual level too. The exact profile will differ for each coachee. That said, we shouldn't be surprised to find some common issues. After all, most of us tend to have similar, multiple goals, such as to:

- ☐ Be better in our chosen job/professional specialisation.
- ☐ Make (career) progress in our organisation/operating context.
- ☐ Realise ourselves outside of the work environment.
- ☐ Better balance our work and life aspirations and demands.

In the context of executive coaching, the Harvard Business Review reported in 2009 a study based on coaches' reporting of what their coachees had requested (at least once or frequently) during their engagement. It is worth noting that subsequent studies have yielded similar results. The more common coachee requests were for help with:

- Developing capability/supporting career progress
- Acting as a sounding board on a range of organisational/strategic matters
- Addressing derailing behaviour
- Team performance
- Outplacement.

Kauffman & Coutu (2009)

As a list of basic concerns, the study should feel familiar to most of us (whether coach or coachee). While we are likely to turn to training and mentoring for technical skills development, coaching is a clear option to help with the needs on this list.

We should also note that, in this list of *executive support* requests, help with personal issues for coachees was also very common. Try as we might, we cannot (and perhaps should not even try to) delude ourselves that the 'executive' and the 'human' are somehow distinct and well-bounded entities.

11.2.1 Career development and coachee focus

Career progression inevitably shifts a person's focus. When most of us first start work, we are rightly focussed on:

- Our core technical competence (whatever work we choose).
- Logistics and orientation (from getting to/from and in/out of the workplace, through to working out what we do for breaks and on to understanding and complying with the site 'rules' (how things actually get done, whom to meet, whom not to offend etc.)).

We will also look to establish and grow our basic work network. We may change employer/track several times during our working life and each time we move jobs, we have to go back around this loop of focusing on the basics.[3] Most of us do at least become better at it with practice.

If we do well at work – and are suitably ambitious – we will begin to secure progressions/promotion. Each step up is a job move – so see the previous paragraph! But, also, the balance of what we do will change. Early promotions tend to be about technical competence and productivity.

Increasingly, over our career, we will be expected to show competence in sales, management, leadership, people development and in the so-called soft skills. A coachee will bring their particular experience and perspective to their coaching and their focus is likely to align with their career stage.

Shifting the emphasis onto soft skills has a number of interesting impacts:

- The required competence profile shifts (see indicative diagram below, which is simply intended to suggest the relative balance in the profile).
- In most cases, the senior profile will be significantly different from what was expected of us when we started out.
- As we progress, we may not be fully aware how the role – and expectations – change. As a result, our behaviour may not adapt as quickly as it needs to.
- In organisations/sectors with relatively flat hierarchies, the balance may shift starkly and only quite late in our working life. This means that we may not have spent much time developing all those other competences we need.

---

[3] By the way, this is true even if we and a few colleagues walk away to set up our own business. The faces may seem familiar, but our responsibilities and relationships have changed. How things are done probably needs to be different too. At least some of the friction/stumbling early on in a start up can be laid at the feet of failing to recognise that there has been a fundamental change in circumstances.

Even if we had prepared for our progression, the nature of workplace dynamics is such that it may still be changing at a faster rate than we expect.

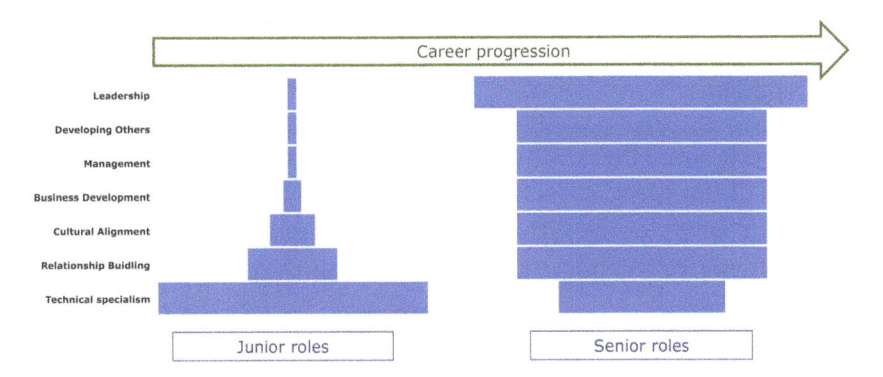

The required competence profile shifts over a career

Together, these impacts can leave those stepping up into leadership roles feeling rather exposed and underprepared. Coaching can thus be an invaluable space for (those becoming) leaders to reflect on and develop their soft skills, away from the expectant glare of their peers and juniors. This is one of the reasons trust and rapport are critical to a strong coaching relationship.

It should be no surprise to find that coachees have a different focus from their employers, or that the focus changes with age, experience and circumstances. The basic principle is that our coachee comes first and we need to understand what they want and support them in their individual journey. The coach may still have to answer to a corporate client too. In practice, therefore, we need to be ready to manage multiple focuses in the coaching relationship.

11.2.2 Being seen – the ultimate focus?

Naturally, business coaching begins its focus in the work context. But coachees never stop being the unique individuals they are. We talked in chapter 6 about the importance of being seen. This need is within each of us wherever we are. I believe that, done well, coaching is a tremendously powerful way to be seen. In particular, it can provide:

- ☐ Validation – the coachee is the coach's whole focus in the coaching session. The coachee is without doubt seen, as they are, without censure; and often with an intensity rarely matched elsewhere.

- ☐ Revelation – the coaching environment is one of I suspect a very small number of settings that enable the coachee to see themselves for everything they are; and to come to accept what they see, or to understand what and how they might change.

These benefits may not be articulated in a coachee's personal objectives. They will almost certainly not feature in any corporate metrics applied to the coaching engagement. But they have a visceral, enduring and in the end reaffirming value for individuals that will tend to resonate beyond any immediate professional concern. As coaches, therefore, we serve our coachees well by ensuring that, amid the business, technical or performance focus, we allow space too for them to see and be seen.

Key takeaways

- Corporate clients are very likely to use coaching:
    - To improve organisational performance
    - As part of the employee reward mechanism
    - As remedial intervention for poor individual performance
- Corporate clients may also try to use coaching to drive organisational cultural change. In particular, much workplace culture is shifting away from ergonomics and toward a more collaborative, innovative environment. This places a greater premium on 'soft skills'.
- Coachees' needs change over their work life.
- As coachees take on more senior roles in an organisation, their need to develop effective soft skills increases sharply.
- Coaching is an effective and 'safe' environment for senior staff to explore new skill/competence development.

III

Coaching with 'I' – some of the practical implications

This section drops into some of the more practical aspects of coaching and the question of making a choice – in the light of what we have seen about the brain and its workings. So, we look at:

- ☐ Contracting for coaching. Corporate clients and potential coachees may come to us with a 'clear idea' of what they want to address. Of course we must address that need. But, given what we see of the uncertainty involved with the brain's processes, we must also think about how 'closed' our contract terms are/should be (chapter 12).

- ☐ Getting the coaching work started. Priming the coachee for the work and establishing a baseline to work from can take a bit of time and effort (chapter 13).

- ☐ Making a choice. This looks at some of the more common circumstances in which I think making a choice to engage more consciously would bring us greater benefits (chapter 14).

The themes we discussed in the previous section do help to prepare for the coaching contract and engagement. Remember, though, that they continue to be relevant to contracting and throughout the coaching engagement.

Coaching with 'I' – some of the practical implications

We do not talk much about specific tools and techniques in this section, mainly because there is so much out there already, not least the comprehensive and accessible volume *We Coach* from Passmore et al. For that reason, I shall only dip into the detail of tools and techniques where there are specific points relevant to our discussion.

12
Contracting for coaching

The majority of coaching businesses are small-scale or single-person companies. These small businesses can struggle to thrive at the best of times. The effort required for sales in particular can feel exhausting, as it comes on top of doing the actual work we are supposed to be doing. We need to:

- Manage the networking required. These days we are all expected to have social media presence; and the claim is that social media will help leverage our networking power. Quite a lot of (albeit anecdotal) evidence, however, suggests that, for coaching, at least 90% of sales will come from personal recommendation rather than social media.
- Develop, adapt and land strong, tailored pitches to a whole range of potential coachees. This includes developing supporting marketing materials.
- Deal (though it often feels like 'battle') with corporate procedures, which can involve multiple stages, checks and competitions just to get started.
- Negotiate the contract.
- Work with what can be quite long (corporate) lead times.

Against all that, the temptation is to push on through the contracting stage to have the contract signed and get things going as quickly as possible.

Think again

Coaching with 'I' – some of the practical implications

The line: 'when you assume you make an ass out of u and me' is rarely more relevant than at the contracting stage. Remember there could be at least 4 parties to a contract:

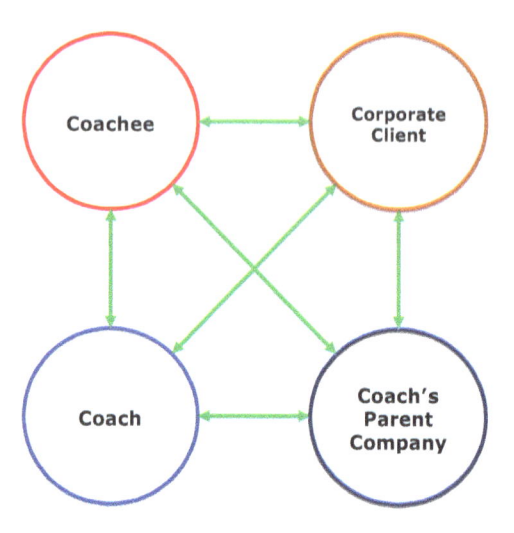

```
    Coachee  ←——→  Corporate Client
        ↕  ╲   ╱   ↕
           ╳
        ↕  ╱   ╲   ↕
    Coach   ←——→  Coach's Parent Company
```

Some of the work in the UK is underwritten by third party funding (government, charities etc.), so there could be additional stakeholders with a clear, vested interest in the outcome of the work contracted. Any or all of these stakeholders – and focuses – may have a key role to play in your coaching engagement.

There is a very good chance that the early exchanges when contracting for coaching will be full of uncertainty. Typically, coachees come to coaching with an agenda. Sometimes this is straightforward. Often, it is not. The picture may be further complicated when you are dealing with a corporate client rather than direct with individual coachees. The basic customer service mantra is to give customers what they want. But I hope we have shown that what is wanted:

- ☐ May not be as obvious as it seems.
- ☐ May be different from what is expected by both/all parties.

- In a corporate relationship, may differ between corporate customer and individual coachees.
- Is likely to have unclear/shifting boundaries.
- May change (quite quickly) once the coaching engagement gets underway.

We have a choice. We can:

- Contract for the requirement as stated, assuming that everybody knows exactly what they want and what they're going to get; and then trust that things will sort themselves out from there, or
- Recognise the uncertainty and risk, especially when contracting with organisations. We can invest sufficient time to ensure that we and our (corporate clients and) coachees have a common understanding of the starting point, joint intention and risk management approach for each coaching engagement. All parties are then better able to contract with confidence and maximum flexibility in their best interests.

I don't expect you will be surprised to hear me argue for the second option.

The sales/contracting phase obviously provides the opportunity to sort out commercial accountabilities. In particular, we typically need to cover off:

- Outputs, outcomes, measures, managing conflict, dealing with absences, terms of business etc.
- Stakeholders' responsibilities and liability for data management. Many companies are still trying to understand fully the implications of the General Data Protection Regulation (GDPR, 2018) and tending to over-protect on or overlook the issue. That does not prevent them, nor you, from becoming liable for improper data handling.

Coaching with 'I' – some of the practical implications

- ☐ Check what more general information security concerns apply. For example, online assessments or online coaching sessions might involve connecting corporate client systems to external sites. While that is relatively common now, you should confirm what constraints/ liabilities apply.

Given our discussion in section II, I hope you will also recognise that the sales/contracting phase offers an invaluable chance to:

- ☐ Clarify initial aims of the stakeholders and establish a clear authority map.
- ☐ Ensure the coach, coachee and corporate client (as appropriate) have the same understanding of:
  - ☐ what coaching is
  - ☐ how it will work
  - ☐ what to expect
  - ☐ confidentiality
  - ☐ why flexibility is required.
- ☐ Assess potential coachee coachability. Yes, this is about the disposition of each coachee, but it is worth reflecting on the extent to which the corporate client is ready for coaching. Have they integrated coaching effectively and positively into their learning and development strategy and practice, for example?
- ☐ Start the process of creating a pattern of making a choice, which prepares coachees for their coaching journey.
- ☐ Assess cultural/ethical fit. This is not about securing a perfect alignment, but there needs to be sufficient fit or both parties will struggle.
- ☐ Start to build trust and rapport.

We can start doing all this from scratch once a contract is up and running. That may be acceptable if everything goes well throughout and the coachee sees the outcomes they wanted and on the terms they expected; and if any corporate client involved is fully satisfied too.

The point is, that in anything other than a perfect scenario, skimping on the matters listed above is likely to cause bigger problems later on, for all involved.

Let's look at some of those matters in a little more detail.

12.1 Stakeholder aims and authority map

The coach, coachee and their sponsoring company will all have a slightly different focus, such as:

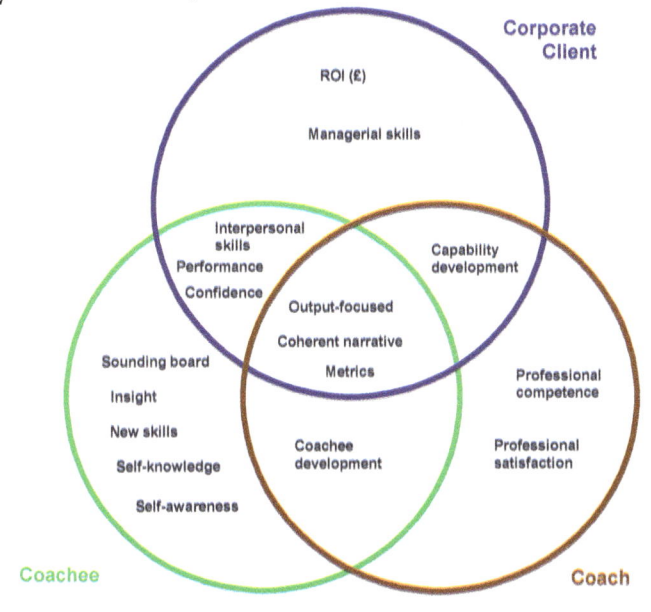

Key outcomes coaches, coachees and sponsoring companies value from coaching (Adapted from de Haan (2019), Kaufmann and Coutu (2009), Kettley and Strebler (1997) and Passmore (2015))

It helps coaches to understand the main stakeholders who have an interest and what those interests are. Knowing this will tell you something about a customer's expectations and their basic attitude towards coaching. In turn, that will help you gauge how much effort you need to put into improving their understanding of what coaching can do for them.

Coaching with 'I' – some of the practical implications

Sorting out authority is important too. Where there is a simple contract between just you and an individual coachee, the lines of authority are clear. I would still argue that you should go carefully through the sales/contracting phase – it will help you both. In my experience, nobody going into coaching for the first time has quite understood its potential landscape or impact. Even a little bit of expectation management can help your coachee focus on getting the most value out of their coaching. It also sets the pattern of the two of you working together to build the solution, which then helps the transition into the coaching relationship.

Authority becomes a more complex and potentially more difficult conversation when a corporate client is involved. Coaching of one or more individuals within a company may attract the interest of:

- The individual(s) themselves
- Their line manager (i.e. the person responsible for overseeing their performance development, providing their annual reports etc.)
- Their task manager – for example, if they are working on a major project, the project manager may have a valid interest in what the coachee is trying to do
- The Commercial team*
- The Finance team*
- The HR team*
- And even board members. If, for example, this is a company's first dip into the world of coaching, interest may well go up to this level.

*In each case, these may be one or more people depending on the organisation's size and structure.

While all of these people may have a valid interest, they may not all have equal or indeed any authority over your contract and how it performs. In contract terms, you have to meet the standards of the contract. Someone (or several people) will have the authority to judge whether standards have been met. Someone (quite possibly a different person) will have the right to authorise payment when the contract is satisfied. This reflects a sensible customer desire to assure output/outcome quality, to sign off completed coaching activity, or to confirm compliance with the terms of the contract. Thus, understanding who has what authority over your contract – and regularly checking that they are content with what is happening – is a key enabling activity for you. It is better all round if contractual authorities and who exercises them (by role at least) are clearly set out in the contract.

In terms of the coachee engagement back into their organisation, I would encourage individual coachees to agree aims and objectives as far as possible with their managers/HR as appropriate. This ensures that all the relevant players are aware of and tied in to the coachee's coaching intention.

12.2 Coachability

Some conditions make it harder than others to support effective coaching with an individual, or in an organisation. In the organisational context, coaching is sometimes used as a remedial measure rather than a developmental one. Being 'sent for' coaching may then be seen as a punishment rather than an opportunity. Similarly, if the organisational culture does not support individual learning, coachees may struggle to make the most of their coaching effort.

At the most basic level, if everybody really is working flat out 24/7, the opportunity for the coachee to rethink and introduce changes into their work environment may be limited. This is not to say that we shouldn't try coaching in difficult environments – far from it. But understanding the nature of the environment will help us support our coachee in developing a more realistic coaching plan.

At the individual level, perhaps the most important factor is whether the coachee has a 'growth mindset' (Dweck, 2008) – in this context, that they believe that they can learn and develop. The coachee's motivation also plays its part – change takes effort and if a coachee is not willing to invest, then progress may be glacial at best.

There are multiple factors affecting coachability. If we step into a contract with inadequate understanding of those factors, we are creating potentially significant risk. It is therefore key to make an effort to understand the context before we start.

12.2.1 Cultural/ethical fit

There does not have to be a perfect fit between you, your coachee or corporate client. Indeed, some differences can be very productive. But there are a few fundamentals to take seriously:

- How much the individual/organisation values learning and development. If there is not a sufficient fit, your coachee's efforts are likely to be undermined, which will demotivate them and potentially damage your reputation.
- Large-scale cultural differences (language, manners, business practices etc.) need to be managed if the coaching experience is to be an effective one.

It is worth noting that a shared language does not ensure a common culture. English, French and Spanish in particular can present some interesting challenges. In each case, there are many non-native speakers who have genuine command of the language. That does not mean that you and they will have a common cultural understanding. This can also hold true for native speakers not from the 'mother country'. Along with areas of cultural overlap, you are likely to find some practical differences too. This can be surprising – the English-speaking nations for example readily fall into the assumption that they have a common language and common culture. As a result, when differences appear, it can catch people unawares – sometimes to dramatic effect.

Cultural differences may also play out at multiple levels. If you have an international organisation as your corporate client, you may be dealing with an overseas corporate entity (and their perspective on learning), a local contract management team (and a different take on performance metrics) and an individual coachee who is from yet another cultural environment.

The key point here is that awareness of the potential for cultural differences affecting the coaching engagement should at least put us on standby. It should encourage us to start a conversation and explore what adaptation might be required.

In similar vein, it is worth taking the time to consider ethical fit. You will have your own position and may indeed be explicitly aligned to a professional code of ethics. Again, there does not have to be a perfect match between you and your coachee/corporate client, but there should be sufficient common ground to underpin your contract.

In this context, therefore, you will want to take a view about the ethical nature of your potential coachee's/corporate client's business and their business practices – and how readily that sits with your own views. Say, for example, that you are fully committed to improving sustainability in all aspects of modern life. That is clearly a good thing. If you want to be active in leading the changes we need, then become a campaigner, become a sustainability coach or consultant, or even become a non-executive director to help shape strategy and practice. We need all of those. Do remember, however, that it is one thing openly offering a specialist service. It is quite another to impose your life/ethical framework on others. So if you are discussing general coaching work with a potential coachee/corporate client who is simply not interested in an issue you hold to be critical – and you find that you can neither accept nor ignore their position – then you should perhaps not work with them as a coach.

12.2.2 Trust and rapport

We have identified a number of potential stakeholders in your coaching engagement (see 12.1). As most of them will have only limited access to your coaching sessions, they have to take it on trust that the coaching investment is worth it... at least until they start to see changes in the coachee(s). Engagement during the contracting phase can help you build trust and rapport with relevant stakeholders and set a positive scene for your coaching work. This will in turn make it easier for coachee(s) to take their learning into the workplace.

12.2.3 Opting out

Sometimes, a coaching relationship doesn't work. This can be for a whole range of reasons – and not anybody's fault. The fact is that although there are things we can do to build trust and rapport, that doesn't guarantee success every time. Coaching is a relationship and relationships can simply fail. It is important, therefore, that you and your coachee are both able to opt out without blame or pain (whether financial or reputational). As appropriate, your corporate client needs to understand and accept this too.

12.3 Commercial accountabilities

You should obviously negotiate basic terms of business (fees and mechanics of payment, professional liability, delays/cancellations etc.). But there are a few other items meriting special care: flexibility, risk, information management and data protection.

12.3.1 Flexibility

It follows from the discussion so far that the shape and focus of an individual coaching engagement is very likely to change over the duration of a contract. Locking down too much detail at the outset risks tying everybody down in lots of bureaucracy for not much reward. Better, if possible, to recognise the potential need to:

- ☐ Change the time and timing of coaching sessions to reflect the work the coachee is doing.
- ☐ Amend aims and objectives as the coachee's understanding and intent evolves.
- ☐ Extend the contract. If the work is focused on a particular outcome or event, for example, it may be best to continue to work through to the date of the expected outcome/event.
- ☐ Finish the contract early. Sometimes the change comes easily. If the focus of the coachee's work was very specific and has been addressed, it may be better all round to end that engagement.

12.3.2 Risk

You are responsible for carrying out basic due diligence on your coachee/corporate client – and they will normally do the same on you. Beyond that, the two main risks are that:

- ☐ You/the coachee are not able to continue the relationship for some reason, e.g. poor health.
- ☐ The relationship with the particular coachee doesn't work. There can be lots of reasons for this, with no blame on either side.

Some upfront agreement on how such things will be managed can save lots of professional and commercial grief later on.

12.3.3 Information management

Again, there are several aspects to consider:

- ☐ Access. With corporate relationships in particular, it may be helpful for you to have access to contextual information, such as performance measurement, reporting criteria and standards.

Coaching with 'I' – some of the practical implications

- Confidentiality. There are several considerations:
    - First is your duty of confidentiality to your coachee(s). This is critical if your coachees are to trust you and so make the most of their coaching investment. However, if a corporate client is involved, they may well assume that they will have access to 'everything' (what is discussed, any notes made by the coach or the coachee etc.). Therefore, agree before coaching starts what access – if any – the corporate client should have to session content. In practice, I have found that if the coachee agrees and reviews progress on objectives with their management and HR, that tends to reassure stakeholders.
    - Second, you are likely to become aware of company information during the coaching engagement. Coachees and corporate clients will no doubt welcome your taking the initiative to show them how such information will be treated in confidence.
    - Material protected by intellectual property rights (IPR) may be shared in sessions. It doesn't matter whether the IPR belong to you, the coachee/corporate client or a third party, they all need to be handled properly. Again, it is useful groundwork to clarify upfront how all involved will handle existing IPR or any new IPR content that emerges from coaching sessions.

12.3.4 General Data Protection Regulation (GDPR)

In one respect, GDPR is just an information management issue. However, understanding and practice is still developing, so there are several things to note here.

- Many countries have legislation to protect the personal data of their citizens/organisations. GDPR is the UK's application of regulations to relevant data being processed within the UK/EU/European Economic Area, or about the citizens of those areas. In other words, for most readers of this book, some form of data protection legislation will apply. Please note: you have liabilities *regardless* of the size of your organisation.

- ☐ For a time at least, you will hold both corporate data (mostly public and general, but some may require more formal handling) and personal data relating to your coachee(s). You need to know and demonstrate to your customers how you will meet your obligations.
- ☐ Your customers will also be expected to manage *your* data appropriately. In most cases, that will include contact data, bank details, the organisation's commercial relationship history with you and, potentially, internal reporting on you as a supplier.
- ☐ In the UK, the Information Commissioner's Office provides relevant guidance for businesses.

Finally, we need to think about metrics.

12.4 Metrics

Coaching brings with it an expectation of change, through better self-understanding, through changing direction/behaviour, through making a choice. Inevitably, when coachees or corporate clients invest in coaching, they will want to understand how effective that investment was. Given a choice, most would love to be able to draw a straight line between investment in coaching and financial notions of Return On Investment (ROI).

Coaching is an expensive and, for seniors/executives, a major business choice. Organisations, and their stakeholders, inevitably expect to see tangible benefit for their development investment and, instinctively, will look to ROI as:

- ☐ An appropriate, business-like measure
- ☐ An approach understood by stakeholders
- ☐ Something that enables comparison with other organisational expenditure.

To that extent, ROI makes a good yardstick and serves senior/executive needs.

In general, coaching seems to do well by this measure, offering strong returns (up to 700% in cash terms claimed in 2009, International Coaching Federation). The evidence also suggests that coaching creates sustained behavioural change (de Haan, 2019), whether that be in terms of communications, overall soft skills, leadership performance etc. That implies that the improved ROI is likely to be sustained.

12.4.1 Why can't we just focus on ROI?

ROI does have its limits, especially in terms of validity and adequacy.

12.4.1.1 Validity: are we actually measuring the ROI impact?

There are technical issues that constrain ROI's validity as a measure. In particular:

- Establishing a robust cause-effect chain between coaching, coachee behaviour and profit outcomes can be difficult. This is especially so if you are trying to identify the full ROI impact of changes in someone's behaviour within a dynamic system (e.g. an organisation, or a set of commercial relationships).

- We need to isolate influencing factors to be sure that coaching – rather than changes in cost profiles or exchange rates, say – caused additional ROI.

- It can be really hard work to frame ROI assessment correctly. Taking measurements means establishing a baseline and a cut-off point – all of that takes time, effort and money. And, as we have seen, the focus of coaching may change once the work is underway. As a result, the original approach to measuring impact in ROI terms may cease to be relevant.

The point is that accurately modelling the impact of coaching in ROI terms may be time-consuming and subject to considerable challenge. We therefore need to recognise that, for most individuals, ROI is at best an indicator rather than an accurate measure. Moreover, there is evidence that a robust focus on ROI creates stress and anxiety, so can be detrimental to individuals and their performance.

12.4.1.2 Adequacy: does ROI capture the true impact?

We also need to think about whether ROI is adequate as a measure. Does ROI really show all the value that individuals and organisations gain from coaching? Things would be simple if it did. But:

- ☐ It's not all about ROI. What if changes in coachee behaviour and performance improve team cohesion and reduce staff churn? What if those changes affect corporate culture – e.g. to be more inclusive or to adapt more sustainable policies and practices?

- ☐ Coachees and corporate clients clearly have something more complex in mind when they think about benefits from coaching. de Haan's studies (2019), indicate that coachees tend to value improvements to insight and self-learning. Corporate clients, meanwhile, often cite changes in coachee behaviour as a clear benefit. These are not outcomes that map readily to an accounting model, yet multiple research exercises confirm that these outcomes (especially in respect of soft skills – Kettley and Strebler, 1997) matter. The point is, whatever the ready utility of ROI, it does not capture many of the impacts that matter to a senior/executive coachee or corporate client.

Capturing non-ROI benefits can be tricky. We have seen that there can be multiple stakeholders in a coaching relationship. It can also take effort to understand what benefit is realised (and where, for example, in the coachee's day to day or a corporate client's organisation). Similarly, identifying the key stakeholder(s) for that benefit and how to capture it in practice can prove tricky. For example, improved sustainability practices can have cost and health benefits for the coachee and their team, but the business as a whole may benefit in market terms – with the Board, Marketing and Finance all potentially able to claim added value.

Whether we are looking to ROI or other benefits, setting the right timeframe for assessment can be a challenge. Some coaching sessions result in instant changes that immediately create benefit. More often, though, the process takes time. A coachee needs to make sense of and internalise the work they have done and then put it into practice and review and learn from their new behaviours. All this means that it can take time for the coachee to see practical benefits – and that corporate benefits are likely to follow sometime thereafter.

12.4.2 The range of non-ROI coaching benefits for senior/executive coachees

There is a significant range of benefits that simply don't fall easily within the idea of ROI, but are clearly valued by stakeholders. Coachees in general value and seek out behavioural change, improved self-awareness and improved leadership competence (de Meuse et al, 2009). They also tend to find greater job satisfaction, better teamwork and improved performance (Williams and Offley, 2005) as a result of coaching. Sponsoring organisations clearly benefit from these changes, even if they cannot turn that into a direct expression of ROI, so it would help them to capture that value too.

Added to all these benefits, seniors/executives look for capability development, improved ability to handle difficult colleagues and for their coaches to act as an impartial sounding board (Kauffman and Coutu, 2009). In practice, one of the more important coaching impacts for seniors/executives seems to be helping them transfer learning to the workplace (Passmore, 2015).

Finally, there is some evidence of physical benefits from coaching. Investigation of the mind-body link suggests there is a powerful interaction between changes in our mental and physical states – aches and pains, for example, can be a physical manifestation of an unresolved challenge (Strozzi-Heckler, 2014). I have certainly found in my own coaching practice then when a coachee fully connects with a way forward, their physical bearing can change dramatically for the better.

The key point is that there can be many non-ROI benefits to coaching for the coachee and their company too, so we need to try to capture those impacts. Broadly speaking, there are two approaches: evidence-based feedback and self-reporting.

12.4.3 Evidence-based feedback

The '360° review', colleague observation (through questionnaires or structured interviews) and performance data (process productivity data, stakeholder engagement data) are perhaps the most common methods of evidence-based feedback. The information generated may be subjective, but it is external to the coachee and reflects impact rather than coachee intent. To that extent, the information is irrefutable and therefore important for development (Albon-Metcalfe and Mead, 2015). Structured approaches are easily repeatable, so can be used to establish baselines and changes over time. There is a risk of a 'Rashomon effect'- differing accounts of the same event, which risks undermining the results. In practice, however, I have usually found that the approaches tend to aggregate to produce a consistent result.

For senior/executive coachees, the more immediate challenge may be accepting the involvement of colleagues in their development – especially if the spark for the coaching discussion was dealing with one's difficult colleagues! As coaches, we should make the case for and keep the focus on the value of evidence-based feedback throughout the early stages of using these tools.

12.4.4 Coachee self-reporting

Coachees widely report valuing what may be seen as 'internal' benefits (self-awareness, confidence etc. – de Haan, 2019), which, by definition, are harder to capture through external observation. But these internal changes have a value in themselves and are a necessary step towards external change (Leedham, 2005). We must therefore turn to the coachees themselves in the quest to identify value. Typical tools here include structured interviews or questionnaires, often using self-scoring tables. Again, the models are repeatable and can help both coachee and coach to track changing perspectives. There is, of course, risk in the subjectivity of self-reporting. It is invariably useful – if at times uncomfortable – for a coachee to explore the detail of their assessment and to make explicit what is happening and its effects. As it accumulates, this evidence can help to sustain an individual coachee in moments of doubt.

12.4.5 Capturing the whole impact

We have briefly reviewed ROI, evidence-based feedback and self-reporting as methods for evaluating the impact of coaching. All three approaches offer useful data, but there is little overlap between them and none individually captures all benefits that coachees have identified. A scorecard approach gives a more complete and more coherent picture of the impact coaching is having. For me, Leedham (2005) takes this a useful step further, by identifying a Coaching Benefits Pyramid, which reflects the fact that change begins with process, then internal changes before becoming visible and having an impact on the coachee's environment. The basic pyramid proposes a stack of:

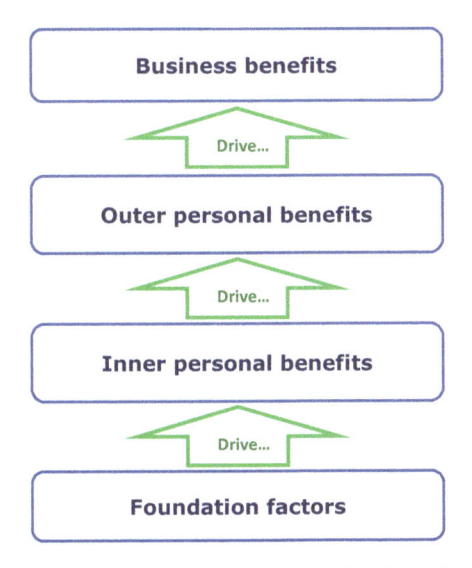

```
        ┌─────────────────────┐
        │  Business benefits  │
        └─────────────────────┘
                 ▲
              Drive...
        ┌─────────────────────┐
        │ Outer personal benefits │
        └─────────────────────┘
                 ▲
              Drive...
        ┌─────────────────────┐
        │ Inner personal benefits │
        └─────────────────────┘
                 ▲
              Drive...
        ┌─────────────────────┐
        │  Foundation factors │
        └─────────────────────┘
```

Coaching Benefits Pyramid, adapted from Leedham (2005)

Here, the coaching environment and activity (Foundation factors) drive changes to coachee confidence and motivation (Inner benefits), which in turn affect behaviour (Outer benefits) and lead to benefits that can be seen in the coachee's business environment (Business benefits). For me, because coachee and business benefits are clearly linked, this helps the coachees themselves and their engagement with their organisations. The pyramid/scorecard approach helps create a change story with inbuilt milestones/measures, which reinforces coachee development.

We should also note the value to coaches too, as the narrative and measures help build evidence for the value of their own practice (Carter and Peterson, 2015).

Given such a rich picture of potential benefit, a narrow focus on ROI seems not entirely helpful. It is probably more effective for most coachees and corporate clients to develop a balanced scorecard to track benefits. This is more obviously compelling when dealing with corporate clients, but there is merit in a similar, if scaled down

Coaching with 'I' – some of the practical implications

discussion with individual coachees too. The scorecard should include a variety of measures, such as:

- ☐ Financial performance data – ROI, efficiency improvements (expressed in cash terms), cost reduction (including indirect costs such as lower HR costs through reduced churn).
- ☐ Behavioural/cultural data – such as reduced staff churn, changes to processes, shifts in morale (through e.g. staff surveys).
- ☐ Coachee-specific data – such as developing leadership capability, improved communications, improved decision-making.
- ☐ Client perspective data – primarily through peer reporting.
- ☐ Other key markers – such as improved compliance, recognition, added brand value.

The key merits to developing a scorecard jointly are that it:

- ☐ Reinforces the breadth of impact that coaching can have.
- ☐ Encourages the coachee to identify and act on scope for change on multiple fronts.
- ☐ Helps the coachee commit to change, because they have developed and own the metrics in their scorecard.
- ☐ Can enhance both the corporate client's and the coachee's view on what they are trying to achieve and so help refine their aims, objectives and metrics.
- ☐ Provides a comprehensive basis for establishing contracting performance terms.

In practice, the balanced scorecard approach is more resilient in handling changes to individual coachee objectives. A coachee with problems in their team may want to be better at dealing with difficult staff. They may discover, however, that simply changing how they communicate achieves the better outcome they wanted. Their focus can then shift to improving their communication skills. The detailed personal objective can easily be updated, but will still contribute to the higher-level aim of improving team dynamics.

Metrics love to multiply and the effort they require can easily escalate. I have gone into some detail here in order to set the scene and to stress the importance of having metrics that are valid, i.e they measure what they claim to measure. But a further key principle with metrics is to keep them brief and simple as possible.

With that in mind, I have included overleaf a sample form for an individual coachee, adapted from the Leedham model. Terms can be difficult: words like 'goals' and 'objectives', for example, can set off a variety of negative reactions. I've used 'milestones' instead, but the idea is the same: agree what you're trying to achieve and why (the 'why' helps with motivation), and the evidence needed to show progress – with SMART (Specific – Relevant – Measurable – Realistic – Timely) measures attached.

There should also be a completion date and a note of key stakeholders on the scorecard. Building a corporate scorecard would be more involved, but the principles of the approach should be the same.

Coaching with 'I' – some of the practical implications

Coaching Balanced Scorecard for: **Period covered:**

Benefits	Focus	Milestone	Why this?	Evidence required	Measures	Stakeholders	Completion date/status
Inner personal benefits	Confidence			This is likely to be based on reporting by the coachee and their peers/teams. Baseline and periodic 360 reviews can provide a consistent benchmark. For self-reporting, a simple coachee scoring mechanism (out of 10) plus some commentary will usually work. Coachees sometimes need prompting to opt for realistic shifts in scores in a reporting period.			
	Motivation						
	Clarity and focus						
Outer personal benefits	Skills			I would encourage coachees to maintain a self-reported profile. It's good practice and can help with annual reviews. If an organisational or professional competence model exists, coachees should try to use that framework directly or as a reference point. Again, baseline and periodic 360 reporting can be useful here. With some competences, reference to professional bodies or certification may be useful.			
	Competence						
	Behaviours						
Business benefits	ROI			This will be the most visible set of outcomes and metrics. When a corporate client is involved, it is important to be clear about the timeframes involved and cause-effect trail between coachee performance and the metrics used (so, careful agreement on contribution to ROI is recommended). If a narrative rather than scoring mechanism is used (which may apply for example to impact on the corporate brand) then agreeing some form of scale and benchmark is helpful.			
	Teamwork						
	Innovation						
	Morale						

We have focussed mainly on the coachee and corporate client interest here, but, to close this chapter, I want to draw attention to the lower end of the Leedham pyramid (Foundation factors). The focus there is on the coaching environment, process and what the coach brings to the table – and how all that helps to add value. In other words, to support both our coachees' and our own development, we are actively encouraged as coaches to:

- ☐ Include ourselves in the metrics discussion
- ☐ Seek feedback on our performance and its impact
- ☐ Reflect on our impact, both alone and in supervision.

This is clearly good practice for us and our coachees.

Coaching with 'I' – some of the practical implications

> **Key takeaways**
>
> ☐ Many of us find contracting difficult and dull, so are keen to rush it. We mustn't. The contracting stage is critical to framing, driving and protecting the coaching relationship.
>
> ☐ Recognising that the coachee position is often uncertain, we need to contract to deal with uncertainty and flexibility.
>
> ☐ There will be multiple stakeholders in the coaching relationship. Use the contracting stage to identify and address those who have responsibility for/authority over the relationship.
>
> ☐ Be sure that both corporate client and coachee are in the right place. Their practical capacity, commitment, cultural/ethical fit and trust/rapport with you all need to be sufficient to make the relationship work.
>
> ☐ Address commercial liabilities upfront, in particular scheduling, risk, information management and metrics. You can't 'fix' these later if things have gone wrong.
>
> ☐ Agree a balanced scorecard for financial and behavioural metrics. This helps corporate clients and coachees acknowledge and act on change on multiple fronts.

13
Getting the coaching work started

The transition from sales and contracting activity into doing the work can be a little bit messy. For both coach and coachee there is value in marking the transition. A habit of agreeing a 'contract' for each session helps put both parties in the right frame of mind. It also helps to have – and to have thought about – core information about the coachee or corporate client (where appropriate) before you start the main sessions.

13.1 Establishing a baseline

It is tremendously helpful to develop a baseline profile of a coachee before formal coaching begins. This work can do a number of useful things, it:

- Kickstarts the coachee into taking time to think about who they are, what matters to them and what concerns them.

- Helps the coachee to identify potential strengths and gaps. Most people find it easier to see what is working well/less well when they externalise their thinking.

- Helps to identify possible inconsistencies or even conflict. Individual coachees may see these for themselves as they work through the baseline exercises. However, because the information is now externalised, it gives the coachee the opportunity to note and reflect on issues of potential interest.

Coaching with 'I' – some of the practical implications

- For coachees who are not used to reflecting on themselves in this way, the tools that coaches use to build the baseline can provide a useful framework and language to help them articulate their thinking.

There are lots of ways to start building a detailed profile of an individual coachee. Broadly, we can look to the following, either individually or in combination:

- Coachee self-assessment. It is good practice to invite a coachee to set down something of their background, their values, their aspirations – and more specifically their goals – the challenges they are grappling with and how they like to work.
- Peer feedback. There is often a difference between how we think we are with others and how they see us. Obtaining peer feedback, such as a manager's report or 360° degree review, can provide a useful alternate perspective.
- Assessment tools. These generally provide holistic or feature-specific profiles. The point is to use the most relevant ones for what the coachee is trying to achieve.

You will realise that some of these tools can be applied both to support a baseline profile and, as we saw in the previous chapter, monitor changes over time for evidence and reporting purposes.

13.1.1 Which baseline tools to use?

There seems to be an endless supply of these and perhaps the first priority for the coach is to focus on the best options for their coachee. It also helps to keep the list brief – too many can become unwieldy for the coach, overwhelming for the coachee.

The range includes:

- Overall personality assessments. Some are preference based (e.g. Myers Briggs Type Indicator®), others more trait based (SDI, DISC®, Thomas PPA®). *Preference-based* tools focus more on the inner individual, *trait-based* focus more on the individual's behaviours. Those with appropriate accreditation may also use 'Big 5'/OCEAN based assessments. Although there appears to be a wide range of assessments, it is worth noting that the great majority of them are underpinned by the same theory, going back about 2,500 years. The ideas were modernised and re-energised in particular by Jung, whose influence is clear in the more popular models. Personally, I find it helpful to use both preference- and trait-based assessments as they tend to drive a more productive dialogue.

- Interaction assessments – based on concepts in e.g. Emotional Intelligence or Transactional Analysis. These focus on particular aspects of thought and behaviour in response to a range of situations.

- Mindset assessments. These focus on e.g. attitudes to learning, values, beliefs, drivers etc. and help to expose some of the more strategic patterns the coachee relies on. In particular, the output of these assessments can help identify inconsistencies or conflicts (e.g. working in a situation that conflicts with our core values). At a practical level, information on learning styles helps the coach to tailor learning options and exercises to meet a coachee's need.

Some more focused assessments may be useful too.

Wherever the coachee's coaching work will take them, coachee and coach should agree a starting focus and objective, which may include input from a corporate client. The agreed focus and objective will typically shape the information we bring together to start coaching. So, for example, if the coachee is looking to improve their leadership skills, then some initial mapping of their relevant skills and mindset is going to be helpful. Similarly, if the coachee is focused on future choices or feeling in conflict in their current situation, a better understanding of their values and drivers may be a higher priority.

13.2 Completing an assessment

The first task is to discuss with the coachee (and, as appropriate, their corporate client) the rationale for assessments; and to agree the particular assessments to be done. Again, this is partially about reinforcing the point that this is the coachee's journey, but it is also about the coachee engaging and committing to the process. Coachees can be quite sensitive about 'being assessed', especially where they sense that some impersonal system is passing judgement on their character. In this context, it generally doesn't matter whether that judgement is positive or negative. Either way, it is important to help the coachee see the assessment as a tool that will help them in their journey rather than a pass/fail test.

The coach then needs to manage the overall process. These days, the great majority of assessments start with questionnaires completed online. A report is produced for the coachee, though it is normally sent via the coach. It is really important that the report is not simply handed to the coachee to make of it what they will.

In addition to any sensitivities the coachee may have, personality assessment reports tend to include a lot of jargon; and some of them take quite strong positions on various behaviours, even if they do not say so explicitly. A key role for the coach, therefore, is to help their coachees understand and explore assessment reports effectively and constructively.

With peer review material, the coachee may be tempted to try to work out the authors of individual comments. I say 'may', I don't think I have ever run a peer feedback review without at least one declaration of: '[insert name here] said that'. Author spotting in itself will generally not be helpful. It can, however, be informative for the coachee to explore their motivation for identifying sources of comments (which is often linked to judgments about others, their relationships with others, or perceptions about their own status within a group).

This feedback process can take time and coaches should allow for that in their planning. It may also take some individual coachees a while to absorb and process all the information generated by the assessments they do. As a result, the coaching dialogue may return to aspects of the assessments over several sessions.

Do keep track of which assessments/items most resonate with the coachee (they may prefer Transactional Analysis language to Thomas PPA® for example). The language imagery of the resonant tools often gives the coachee a helpful, more objective frame of reference and language when analysing situations/challenges; and reinforces the coachee's understanding and use of the assessment.

13.2.1 Handle with care

The question of coachee sensitivity about personality assessments is worth further thought. 'Personality' is another of those terms we happily use, but defining it proves to be difficult in practice. There are several versions and variants on the concept, but at least a broad convergence on the idea that personality is about patterns of thought (and emotion) and behaviour. To that extent, there is clear convergence on our concept of 'I' – which we already know is tricky to nail down. If neither 'I' nor 'personality' are clearly defined, we won't be surprised to find that any boundary between the two ideas is hazy too.

My own current 'line of best fit' thinking when talking this through in the coaching context is that:

- ☐ 'I' is about *who* I am (so includes the totality of thought, feeling, action, memory, conscious and subconscious)

- ☐ 'Personality' is about *how* I am (the more persistent thought, feeling and action related to my engagement with 'other'). There is a lot of discussion out there, though, about just how persistent, consistent and context-dependent personality might be.

Coaching with 'I' – some of the practical implications

It seems to me that personality is in some sense an aggregate/fusion of several factors:

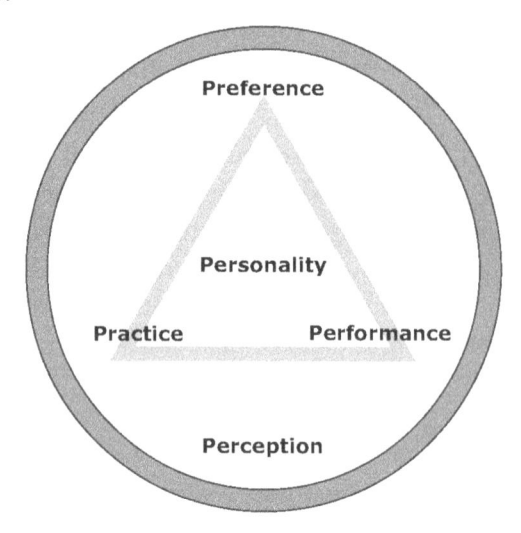

Diagram: A circle containing a triangle. Labels: Preference (top), Personality (centre), Practice (bottom-left), Performance (bottom-right), Perception (bottom).

Where:

- Preference – the patterns of thought/behaviour we want to apply
- Practice – the patterns of thought/behaviour we actually apply (and these may vary with context)
- Performance – how competently we act
- Perception – this is twofold: first, our own perception of our personality and the alignment of our preference, practice and performance; second, other people's perception of those things.

The point about alignment is a telling one. We may be one of those happy individuals who is genuinely aligned in how we want to engage the world, how we actually engage with it and in the competence of our actions; we may know all this and those around us may see it too. This happy state is technically possible. However, I suggest that the reality for most of us is that we don't always practise what we preach; practice doesn't always make perfect (nothing I do now will ever make me a world-class ballet dancer, even if I wanted to do that); and the way I see me is often different from the way others seem to see me. Some aspects of these gaps will only be recognised by our subconscious selves – but the knowledge is locked in there. In other words, for most of us, there are gaps between the aspiration and the reality of our personality.

So, when coachees come to work through a personality assessment, there are risks. They may sense that the assessment:

- ☐ Is sailing pretty close to examining their inner self ('I') – which can feel deeply exposing for some.

- ☐ May expose inconsistencies and gaps between how they wish to be and what happens in the world.

- ☐ Will draw them into discussion about 'soft skills' (since so many assessments have a strong focus on interaction with others), which may be a (known/perceived) weakness for them.

- ☐ May invite discussion about their competence in some areas. Someone may prefer to think 'big picture' and practise 'staying above the detail', but if they haven't learned and invested in the techniques of strategic thinking, critical analysis etc., their 'big picture' may be comprised of quite a bit of fog. For another seemingly common example: a coachee may think they are 'people' focused, but practise effective communication rather less than they realise. They may then be shocked to learn that others' perception of their communication competence (and as a result, their personality) is rather more bleak than their own.

As coaches, we need to recognise that assessments can stir up a lot of thoughts and feelings, most of them useful, if not always welcomed by coachees. It is therefore important that we handle them with care. We need to set the assessment exercise up carefully – and be clear about the gains that come from the process. We also need to ensure that coachees have the right time and support for them to work through the assessment reports, including what's comfortable in the assessment and what's challenging.

Coaching with 'I' – some of the practical implications

I have found that coachees feel strongly (irresistibly?) drawn to the presumption that because they have a strong preference/practice in a given area, their performance there must be strong too. It is usually worth the effort to maintain the distinction between preference, practice and performance and encourage the coachee to identify evidence of performance. Sometimes the coachee's instinct is right, sometimes they identify a gap. Either way, they are building a robust baseline for themselves.

For many coachees, the personality assessment can kickstart the Recognition condition for learning (see 8.2). Remember that recognition may happen at multiple levels: the situation, the patterns and in particular beliefs, values and drivers at play, the coachee's role in and responsibility for how things are. That can be a powerful process, sometimes too powerful. Again, therefore, we need to handle the process with care.

13.3 Resisting the answer

The coach can end up with a lot of detailed, rich information about their coachee and the coachee's organisation. The vast majority of coaches also tend to have built up some prior work experience (and, with that, some biases). A coach may therefore find themselves faced with the overwhelming temptation to conclude that they 'know' the answer for their coachee. After all, there could be some clear signals.

Take the following example, where a coachee has completed a self-report and assessments on values, drivers and traits. The coachee has indicated that:

- ☐ Their highest value is social recognition. They also gave relatively high scores to helpfulness, responsibility and being obedient.
- ☐ Their key drivers are to work hard, to please others and to be perfect.
- ☐ They tend to try to fit in at work, avoid conflict, take the safe career options.

Getting the coaching work started

- They are currently feeling exhausted. They're doing too much, working long hours, six days a week. They seem to be doing a lot of work for other people and can never say 'no' when asked to take on more. Yet, for all the high-quality work they do, they never seem to get promoted; and they have just missed out in yet another promotion round. They're feeling rejected, something of an outsider – they think they are simply not good enough. They are struggling with their work environment and feel tired all the time, whether at work or at home. All told, they now feel they've reached an impasse. Worse, they've been here several times before. They know that things need to get better, but they don't know how.

As coaches, we will no doubt see a strong reinforcement pattern at play:

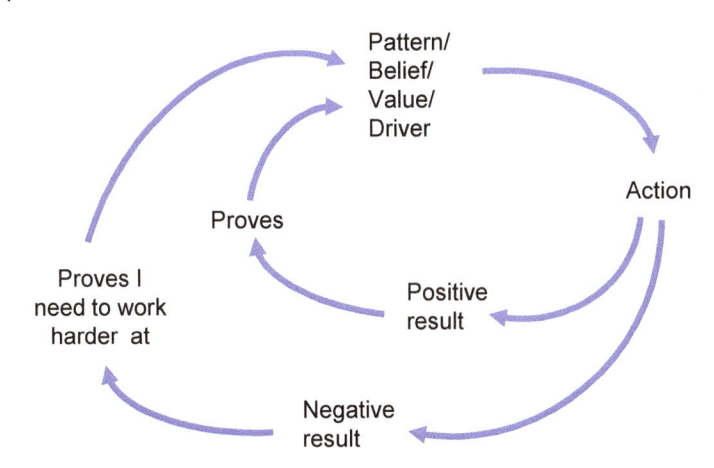

[Diagram: A cyclical reinforcement pattern showing Pattern/Belief/Value/Driver → Action → Positive result → Proves → back to Pattern; and Action → Negative result → Proves I need to work harder at → back to Pattern/Belief/Value/Driver]

There are clearly lots of starting/entry points for discussion here and we will almost certainly have seen some of this before either in our own or others' experience. We will likely have a view on what's been happening – and what will happen. Many of us will have slipped seamlessly into a view that we understand the problem and the answer for our coachee.

Think again.

Coaching with 'I' – some of the practical implications

This is the coachee's situation, not ours. Their challenge, its importance and its solution are what they make of them in their context. We don't yet know what patterns or evidence underpin their thinking. In particular, we don't know what lies behind the beliefs, values or drivers shaping their thoughts. Thus, not only do we not know what factors are in play, we do not understand the thread from belief to action, say, that our coachee will need to trace in order to rethink their position. The coach's role is to support the coachee in working through these questions. Imposing on a coachee what we think is best for them – however well-intentioned – is likely to get in the coachee's way. In fairly short order, both coach and coachee would find that dialogue frustrating and unproductive.

We have some useful learning for ourselves here:

- ☐ We can see a lot of potentially interesting challenges and threads that the coachee may pursue.
- ☐ We may resonate with aspects of their experience.
- ☐ We can see that our insights will help us come up with useful questions/challenges when the right opportunities present themselves.
- ☐ We have identified experiences that we can share with the coachee if they invite us to; and which may give them a different perspective on their challenge.
- ☐ In fairness, we may even be at least partially correct in what we think.

Our experience may also leave us well-placed to act as mentor to our coachee – and that may be valuable to them. However, it is important that we are:

- ☐ Clear that we have good (not just convenient) reason to mentor (remember: that's about transferring knowledge) instead of coach.
- ☐ Explicit when we shift into or out of a mentor role.

Getting the coaching work started

☐ Mindful of the constraints of the contractual arrangements we have in place with the coachee (and corporate client).

Knowing the answer for a coachee seems to be one of the more persistent and pernicious traps for coaches. The vast majority of us seem to struggle with it at some point and may become concerned about whether we are doing the right thing by the coachee. Working through a coachee's set of assessments is one of those points in the coaching relationship when we may be most drawn to declaring an answer. But, at this stage, we are usually just applying some of our own framing and availability patterns (i.e. using our experience as a frame and treating the assessments as a complete statement of the situation). Knowing the risk, we must work to resist the answer.

13.4 Using media effectively

We also ought to think about the venue of coaching sessions. For a variety of reasons, we have turned more and more to online meetings over the last 10 years. The arrival of COVID-19 only served to accelerate that process. There is clearly some value to the virtual meeting:

☐ Coach and coachee can be more or less anywhere in the world and yet still 'meet'.

☐ The logistics tend to be easier. One or both parties do not need to travel. We may not need to book scarce meeting rooms in busy offices, or spend time travelling.

☐ Going virtual makes it easier to connect outside normal working hours.

The virtual option, however, is not necessarily a clear winner. Fairly consistently over the last 30-40 years, computer-mediated interactions have been shown to be less effective than physical ones. Many people find it harder to focus for any period of time and that they are much more easily distracted when working on screen. There does also seem

Coaching with 'I' – some of the practical implications

to be a difference in experience depending on whether virtual attendees have met in person beforehand. The reasons for all this are not fully understood, though they seem to go back to a point we considered earlier on.

As we know, the brain engages all its senses (be it 9 or 55) to make sense of 'other'. So, when we go virtual and work with the screen instead of a live human (!), we lose some 78-96% of the sources of data we would normally receive in a face-to-face meeting. We are stuck with limited sight and sound input, trying to fill in all the blanks (approximation again) that would normally be filled by the rest of our senses. This may create a number of effects:

- We are less engaged because there is less information coming in.
- Because the brain recognises the information deficit, it devalues what information it does receive.
- If the brain is trying to compensate for the information deficit, then it may be working harder, tiring sooner and so less able to sustain interest and attention.
- With less information available, we find it harder to 'read' the other person, which is alienating as well as tiring. It also means we are more likely to misunderstand what they are trying to say.

We can to some degree compensate for these factors. We can activate more senses and improve engagement in a virtual coaching session by asking how something feels, where it is in relation to the coachee, even talking about tastes and smells where relevant. It can be tempting to call on a range of audio-visual gimmicks to compensate – with fancy slideshows, dramatic graphics and stirring music. These distractions often receive favourable comments, but we should be wary about assuming that means that adequate connection, or our point, has been made. Virtual means 'nearly/almost'. We might do well to keep in mind that 'nearly communication' is clearly missing something.

Some effort to compensate for the alienating effects of remote/virtual communication can help, but there is no escaping the fact that we have to work harder to build a human connection when we go virtual. For that reason, we should try to have at least some in-person meetings, especially early on in the relationship.

If a virtual meeting is somehow lesser than a physical meeting, telephone meetings take us further away from natural human contact. Text and email support drift us further apart again. As distance grows, so does the risk of misunderstanding/miscommunication. So, as a basic approach when using telephone/email contact to support ongoing coaching work:

- ☐ Use telephone/mail support only once the relationship is established. Once there is some familiarity between coach and coachee, there is likely to be less scope for misunderstanding.

- ☐ Use telephone/mail support to focus on *brief and specific factual points* (confirming use of a technique) or reassurance. It is too easy to miss the detail/thread in long exchanges.

Coaching with 'I' – some of the practical implications

Key takeaways

- ☐ Building a baseline coachee profile is an important first step to get started with coaching.

- ☐ Baselines should aim to explore background, aspirations and goals, mindset (e.g. values, drivers, readiness for coaching, learning style) and personality.

- ☐ Some coachees see personality assessments as intrusive. It is therefore important to show our coachee how any tool we want to use will help them.

- ☐ The tools that most resonate with a coachee can often provide an objective frame of reference and language which help them articulate their thoughts and feelings.

- ☐ The baseline profile is a rich source of information and will provide useful clues for a coach, but we must resist the temptation to jump to conclusions about the coachee's needs.

- ☐ Virtual meetings (and indeed other media) are useful for a variety of reasons, but they are never quite the same as 'physical' meetings. Using IT/social media works best once coach and coachee have established their relationship. Even then, it is better to keep telephone/mail/text exchanges brief and factually focused.

14
Common challenges

In this chapter, we home in on some of the more common challenges that coachees are addressing – and how as coaches we support their response. The particular emphasis here is the coachee moving into making a choice about ownership and action. Rather like chapter 3, my intent is to offer a 'starter' catalogue of circumstances where a coachee is trying to make a choice. So, it is not an exhaustive example set, but I hope puts some of the ideas around making a choice into a practical coaching setting.

14.1 Making a choice

In essence, making a choice is about taking control. It is about stepping back towards conscious competence. Or, depending which model works for you, it is about putting System II or the Human in charge. This is an act of will that takes effort.

It begins with that first making a choice to act. Some people will then make a choice to begin coaching in order to help them change their thinking/practices. Within the coaching environment, the challenge is to help our coachees make more choices about specific situations, opportunities or risks. It is also about helping them decide for themselves how best to manage the balance of automatic and deliberate thinking in their day to day lives.

To remind you, the point is not to argue for wholesale change – a life of constant, complete awareness would be unbearable for most people. But if everyone made even a modest degree of change (placing maybe 2-5% more of their decision-making into their conscious processing), that could have a dramatic impact. In particular, focusing in on identifying the kinds of decision(s) that they recognise as important and working harder to make conscious choices in those spaces will further increase the impact on their lives.

14.1.1 Tackling the basics

As we saw earlier, there seems to be a basic cognitive cycle at work in the brain:

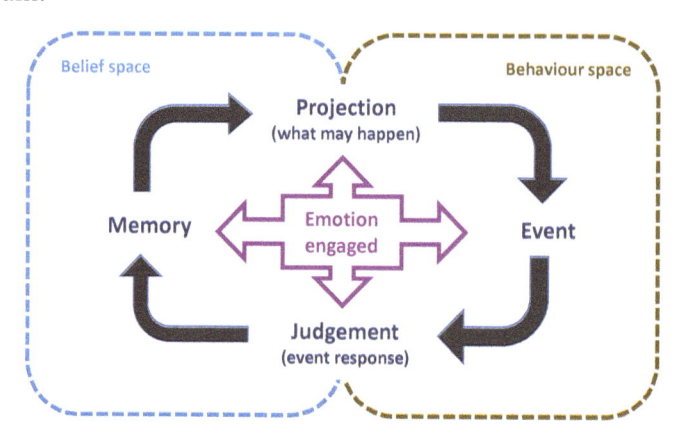

```
Belief space                          Behaviour space
              Projection
              (what may happen)
                   ↑
   Memory ← Emotion engaged → Event
                   ↓
              Judgement
              (event response)
```

Over time, we each build up a library of patterns – some simple, some complex – to help us cope with the fast and constant stream of data that we must manage. Most of the time, this cycle works on automatic. Most of the time, we are content with this, because the cycle and its patterns get it right – or at least sufficiently correct for our purposes. But we've also seen that:

- ☐ The brain can unwittingly make mistakes.
- ☐ Patterns are not always useful in every circumstance.
- ☐ The increasing complexity of our world encourages the brain to make more use of those patterns. At the same time, that complexity challenges the validity of many of the patterns the brain has become used to relying on.

At the practical level, this means that one of the more useful learnings for coachees making a choice, is to develop their ability and capacity for constructive reflection. There are several tools out there (e.g. NLP, CBT) to explore and use as makes sense for you and your coachee. In essence, a general model for *CHOICE* would focus on:

- Conditions. Identify levels of decision that matter and the circumstances associated with those decisions. This helps coachees identify *before* they make a choice that a key decision is surfacing and needs their attention.
- Hitting pause. This is about a coachee invoking their conscious self (System II or Human) to take control of what they do next.
- Outlining the situation – including awareness of the emotions they have attached to the situation.
- Investigating their thoughts and feelings. What patterns might be in play? Are they appropriate? What alternate options do they have?
- Choosing the option that will work for them in the situation they face. This may be 'carry on as you were' – their patterns may be serving them well – or it may be time to change/replace a pattern. Either way, they are now giving themselves a chance at evolving a more appropriate, more effective way forward.
- Enacting their chosen option. Coachees should also evaluate how things went afterwards – this will improve (or show them they must reject) the pattern they have used.

The model set out here is scalable – it can be as intensive and extensive as it needs to be. It is something that coachees can apply in any circumstance. Having a fairly simple model to use will help them establish a level of control and good practice.

Coachees can readily build a pattern of healthy doubt and constructive reflection. They do need to understand, however, that changing or replacing a pattern requires effort over time, both to delete the old

Coaching with 'I' – some of the practical implications

pattern and to establish a new one. The more an existing pattern is rooted in the 'deeper' stuff, the more time and effort it may take to shift. Similarly, the more radical a new pattern, the longer it may take to adopt. Note that where a challenge lies within a tied pattern (remember: where several patterns may cluster to form an abiding preference/trait), the coachee may need to work on more than one individual pattern in order to make progress.

As coaches, we need to remember the importance of gathering and reviewing evidence in order to support the coachee throughout the process.

14.1.2 Potential blockers

The logic of better decision making seems quite straightforward. In practice, however, it can prove surprisingly challenging. Inertia can be a factor, but there are some other unhelpful influences out there too.

Sometimes, a coachee's concern may be less about the nature of the choice than a reluctance to make a choice at all. Choices are generally by their nature decisive. That means that dealing with uncertainty and risk – and therefore stress – are part of the situation. Indeed, the uncertainty, risk and stress may be the main issue(s) for a coachee. As we know, stress provokes chemical activity in the brain which can then impair its normal functioning. For some coachees, the challenge will then be first to deal with the stress, but then to see beyond that and into the potential for change. They may need to break the challenge down into smaller chunks, so that the amount of stress associated with each chunk is manageable.

Some curious thinking patterns can scupper an attempt to make a choice. A coachee may come to coaching with a focus on a job offer, or problems with a member of their team that seem straightforward. Yet they struggle to move forward:

- ☐ For some, the decision is difficult because making a choice one way can exclude other options, which they are reluctant to lose.

- Others jibe at the responsibility of taking the decision. Those who rely on 'intuition' alone may struggle to make a call between choices of apparently equal value.
- For some, the difficulty lies in a conflict between head and heart over what to do.
- For others, lack of critical/analytical thinking skills may be the root of the problem.

The point in each of these cases is that, to make progress, the coachee will need to focus on these issues rather than the whatever starting point they brought to their coaching. However, we mustn't rush them and propel them into where we think the issue lies. A coachee will often need to work through their initial concern in order to get to what really matters. The CHOICE, or any other reflection model, will only come to serve them well if they trust it and use it with their own hands.

14.1.2.1 With or around emotion?

As we have seen, emotion is a critical part of our core cognitive cycle. In some circumstances, the emotional attachments to a memory or a pattern can be overwhelming. If the attachment is strong enough to cause trauma, then the coachee should be encouraged to seek support from an appropriate therapeutic professional.

At lower thresholds, emotional attachments can be motivating ('I won't do that again!', 'I'll get it right next time!'). Such thoughts can also still get in the way, though. Whether the association feels positive or negative, if it is too dominant, then it will distort a coachee's thinking on a choice. Some practitioners prefer to help coachees desensitise as a response, but it may be more helpful to learn to work with, rather than despite, an emotional attachment.

One option here is to help coachees learn to observe rather than simply re-live emotional experiences. A simple visualisation technique invites the coachee to recall a relevant emotionally charged event; and to recall the emotion they attached to it. When they have that scene and feeling(s) clear in their head, they then imagine themselves floating up above the scene until the point where they no longer feel the associated emotion. At this point, they can cast a more objective eye on the event and its importance. This is when they can start to rethink the value of the memory/pattern they are working with and move into a more balanced place where they can make a choice. Importantly, this technique does not seem to interfere with the original emotional attachment – so that the emotional energy remains available to a coachee if they should need it (e.g. for motivation).

14.1.2.2 Sticking at it

Achieving and sustaining motivation can prove a difficult hurdle. Remember that creating, changing or replacing a pattern takes more energy, so the brain may naturally struggle to keep at it. This underlines the importance of *Support* (see 8.2) in the coachee's learning/changing process. As coaches, we are often a key element of our coachee's support mechanism.

14.1.2.3 Engaging in the process is making a choice

Finally, we should keep in mind that the coaching process itself is framed by – and suffused with – making a choice. Engaging a coach in the first place is a shift for any coachee. The three intentions – expose, explore, evolve – also entail making a choice. Evolve seems obvious: we are making a choice to change. When we undertake to expose or explore, we are also making a choice to see and be seen as we are. That can feel challenging for many, underlining why coachees need to be able to trust their coach.

14.1.3 Common challenges

Let's now take look at some of the more common challenges identified. We can use the making a CHOICE approach in each case, along with other tools/methods. As we have seen, the presenting issue can be quite different from what is really going on. What may start out looking like

Common challenges

a question of career choice, may turn out to be more about belonging. Similarly, self-sabotaging behaviour may turn out to be about a conflict of ethics or values. We also need to remember that it may take time for clarity about the root of the coachee's concern to surface. So, the groupings below are simply about dialogues with similar features. Please don't assume there are any hard boundaries between them.

14.2 Making a choice about direction

Image by: Javier Allegue Barros on unsplash

The typical scenario here is that a coachee finds themselves looking at a (strategic) choice, be it dealing with an opportunity or risk. With the CHOICE model in mind, the coaching session provides an opportunity to pause. As a starting point, the coachee can make an initial statement of the situation, their perception of it and their feelings about it.

Let's take three common examples of direction choices: stepping into a new role, leaving a job and inner conflict.

Coaching with 'I' – some of the practical implications

14.2.1 Moving on (up)?

If a coachee has doubts about stepping (up) into a new role, they may have concerns about:

- ☐ Their own competence.
- ☐ The impact of the move on their work/life balance.
- ☐ Disrupting existing relationships.
- ☐ Their readiness for new levels of responsibility.
- ☐ Their commitment to the role or the organisation.
- ☐ The life journey they have imagined for themselves.

Each of these concerns is likely to have positive and negative associations. More than one concern (and more than one pattern) may be in play – and distinguishing between them may be part of the challenge. Some concerns may be driven by deep-rooted beliefs. Promotion opportunities, for example, are common triggers for a bout of Imposter Syndrome.

While each concern may be valid, the coachee should find it helpful to test:

- ☐ What evidence there is to support the concern – and whether that reflects a substantive issue.
- ☐ What pattern may be behind the line of thinking – and whether the pattern is really serving them in this instance.

This will help them identify whether to set aside their concerns, or decide on a plan of action to deal with them.

14.2.2 Should I stay or should I go?

There may be several compelling reasons to quit, including:

- ☐ To improve terms and conditions.
- ☐ As an opportunity to grow professionally.
- ☐ Because things aren't working anymore.

Common challenges

In the simpler circumstances, the discussion is more likely to be about leaving well, leaving colleagues behind and/or managing the transitional risk. The drive to leave, however, may be offset by other considerations, such as an easy commute or predictable working hours. A simple weighing of the pros and cons may then help to frame the issue into a manageable decision.

Even the easiest departure involves an element of uncertainty and risk. This may be complicated where the situation is genuinely stressful. A coachee may be trying to reach a decision through the powerful frames of:

- ☐ A fight response, fuelled by frustration and anger – a sense that they have been ill-used and overlooked. Where people see that fight will not work, they tend to turn to
- ☐ A flight response, with an overwhelming need to be elsewhere. Note this may be physical or psychological (people simply 'withdraw' from what's going on).
- ☐ Exhaustion, when they can simply do no more here.

In these cases, a coachee can slip into a pattern of 'away from' thinking and behaviour, doing what they can to end an unhappy situation. But, in their rush to get 'away from', they can lose sight of what they may be moving towards. As a result, they may start running at full tilt in one direction, with their heads firmly turned back to see what's chasing them. That scenario has an almost inescapable conclusion: they are on the way to another fall. In those circumstances, people may take a new job to get away from the old, only to put themselves into a similar, undesired situation. Worse, this scenario can become an established pattern.

Again, it tends to be helpful to coachees if they break up their situation into chunks. Step by step they can then consider their options; make sense of whether to leave (deal with past and present); then work out what to do next (address the future).

Coaching with 'I' – some of the practical implications

14.2.3 I am what I am

Coachees may be facing a sense of conflict within themselves, driven by:

- ☐ Tension between their personal and social values.
- ☐ Dissonance between corporate and their personal values.
- ☐ Dissonance between the values espoused and those practised by employers, colleagues or friends.

Everyone tends to assume that everybody else has the same values they do. As a result, it can be a surprise when this turns out not to be the case. If someone has invested in a relationship and assumed that all involved were of like mind, it may be some time before they realise that important differences exist. Again, this adds to the sense of shock, outrage even, that anyone may experience when they are forced to confront differences.

Organisations have values too. Anyone intending to work for an organisation, would do well to check whether their values and those of their prospective employer fit well enough. It is commonplace now for organisations to make a point of telling us about the values that they espouse. As these declarations are a matter of public record, there is no real excuse for not checking. It may also be worth exploring beyond the corporate website, to try to confirm that the organisation embodies in practice the values it espouses in principle.

The majority of people also tend to assume that they know their own values. This turns out not to be true more often than one might think. In part, this is because people are subject to constant influences on their sense of values. Obviously, home and school have an early and enduring impact, but the influence continues into adulthood, too. Humans are naturally social creatures and, as a result, will tend to conform with their peer groups. Over time, they may lose sight of their personal values through the habit of accommodating others. They may then begin to overlook gaps between their and others' values. As a result, when differences come to light – or even to conflict – it can come as something of a shock to people when they rediscover their real values.

A coachee may have to work through a range of ideas about their values (and where they come from) in order to get to what really worries them. As we have seen, values link into beliefs and are likely to be deep-rooted and emotionally charged. So, challenges here may be uncomfortable to expose, explore and evolve.

As coaches, we should be prepared for any discussion involving values to become complicated and develop over time. We should also be aware that some challenges may be so fundamental and intractable that they go beyond coaching's reach. We need to be mindful of the potential boundary and, if appropriate, help the coachee identify what other support may be beneficial.

14.3 Making a choice about belonging

Image by: pixabay on wiki commons

As we know, humans are a social species, so belonging is a powerful driver for everyone. Control over who belongs is a key attribute of power in groups. As a result, so much (too much) human dialogue is about 'us' and 'them', drawing whatever lines are convenient at the time. Human history is littered with examples of 'othering' strategies –

Coaching with 'I' – some of the practical implications

whether about shunning, excommunication, exile, persecution, social exclusion or, these days, cancel culture – directed at those deemed not to belong.

Where people fear being excluded, they are more likely to comply, even with extraordinary behaviour. Take the example of the experiments run by Milgrim in the 1960s/70s. Subjects were placed in a room with a two-way mirror. They could see another person in the neighbouring room, identified as a learner being asked questions. The subjects were told to press a button to inflict an electric shock on the learner whenever the learner got a question wrong. The intensity of the shock increased at each stage of failure. The learner would respond to the shock given, with apparently growing distress. In theory, the shock would reach levels that would cause permanent harm. Yet a high proportion of subjects continued to press the button as instructed.

In reality, there was no electric shock in the Milgrim experiments. The whole point was to test human willingness to conform, even when that seems inappropriate. There has been lively discussion about the applicability of the experiment since its results were first published. Even so, that basic instinct to conform among the majority of humans – even in challenging circumstances – has been well documented. As a result, coachees may discover they have surrendered to 'the group' much more than they ever realised, or would have wished, in order to belong.

The 'weaponisation' of belonging and exclusion seems to be a constant feature of most cultures. It also means that individuals are likely to be even more sensitive to whether they belong or not. That sensitivity makes it all too easy to mis-read the simplest experiences: they may interpret somebody not turning up to a meeting as rejection, when they had simply failed to check before sending a request that their colleagues don't work on Wednesdays. This may look like a trivial example in black and white, but, in context, this is not as rare a mis-reading as we might assume; and may breed powerful resentment.

Common challenges

Some of the challenges about belonging reflect inner conflicts (as above), but there are other forms too. These often surface as:

- ☐ Issues with team cohesion and performance.
- ☐ Staff conflict/dealing with difficult staff. Though the conversation is often around control and authority, there is typically an emphasis on an individual (or small group) being different from the rest/the 'norm'.
- ☐ Self-sabotage. This is often driven by a person's belief that they don't belong here, are not good enough and will be found out and excluded. They might exclude themselves (from a group, an activity or even an organisation) in order to 'control' the risk of being cast out – even though it typically has a negative impact.
- ☐ Rebalancing our commitments. This tends to manifest as a work-life balance discussion. The simple fact is that there is limited time in the day and most people belong to more than one 'tribe': the team at work, professional bodies, work social groups, non-work social groups, their families. All of these demand time as part of the 'price' for belonging. Periodically, most people need to adjust their time commitments or tribe memberships in order to continue to meet their needs in a balanced and healthy way.

In each of these cases, the coachee may have concluded that they don't belong. Sometimes, however, it may be that coachee has become concerned by others' not belonging (i.e. not conforming with their idea of how one or more colleagues should behave).

14.3.1 Common features in belonging discussions

Several features may appear in belonging discussions:

- ☐ Framing patterns that set the rules of the game. These may be formal, professional or social. They are often not written down, but group members (whatever group that may be) are expected to know them and comply. Much of anyone's early time in a new environment, be it school or work, is focused on understanding and complying with the rules as practised.

- Single perspective frames of communication. Here, a coachee can be locked into one view on a situation, unable to accept any other perspective. Any alternative perspective is then looked on as a challenge. In Transactional Analysis terms, this may be a tendency to dwell in a Parent or Child position as a communicator. In Myers Briggs or NLP terms, everyone tends to communicate from their own point of preference. If they do not use language that resonates with others' preferences, they tend to lose and then alienate their audience. In the professional context, jargon is meant to help groups of people collaborate more effectively. It may do so. But it can also be wielded to powerful effect both to identify 'us' and exclude 'them'.

- Coping with conflicting demands. Different tribes may collide – this could be as simple as the sales and operations teams arguing over pricing. Tribes may also erupt out of an existing tribe. In the search for identity, a lot of the emphasis tends to be on difference, rather than similarity. The tribe 'new' to the situation feels like a challenge to the rest, a threat to the instinct to belong. The resulting noise can make communication so much harder for all involved.

14.3.2 Space matters too

The physical environment can play its part in shaping a sense of belonging. Indeed, I have worked with coachees who changed roles (and employers) precisely because their office environment did not meet their needs.

In many countries, responses to COVID-19 led to asking the majority of people to work from home and many found that they were more productive at home than at the office. Inadvertently, the pandemic reminded everyone that, while some people are more efficient and effective when working mainly in groups, others need quiet space to be at their best.

You might think that a sensible office strategy would be to try to provide a balanced environment to get the most out of all the staff. However, office design of the last few decades has been dominated by open-plan environments. They were claimed to improve connection and productivity, though cost-saving often seemed to feature suspiciously high up in the list of claimed benefits.

With open plan came hot desking, which looked like a great space saver. Yet open plan and hot desking have not been an unqualified success. In some decades of working in open plan offices, I regularly observed significant numbers of people who put in the effort to create a workaround (whether to create group or private spaces) to meet their needs. Of course, time spent securing an effective workspace was time not spent doing the day job. Often, such spaces became reserved for particular groups. As a consequence, the workarounds tended to encourage us/them dynamics between those who established themselves as 'permanent residents' in the office space, and those who were 'visitors'.

Odd though it may sound to us at first, we should not be surprised if coachee discussions about workplace redesign and problems with(in) teams happen in fairly close proximity. Given the potential impact of space, we should remember that if the coachee is able to change their working space, they may be able to improve their sense of belonging at work.

14.3.3 Boundaries

Belonging invokes a sense of boundaries (us/them, in/out). Group members tend to assume that, within their groups, everybody has the same view on what those boundaries look like. In practice, that may not be the case. Indeed, any group member may not be so clear themselves about the boundaries, never mind about the extent to which the group shares a common view.

The belonging discussion often trips up over two words that turn out to be unhelpful a lot of the time, because they create ambiguous boundaries:

Coaching with 'I' – some of the practical implications

- Fairness. Everyone wants fairness, yes? But for some people that means everybody should be treated the same. Others, however, think that fairness means that each person should be treated according to their need. Any effort to reconcile these differing positions in office or organisational policy can lead to things becoming fraught quite quickly. Moreover, determining who should have the right to decide any individual's or group's 'need' can create its own rich vein of conflict.

- Equality. Again, who could argue with that? But for some, equality is about opportunity, for others, it is about equality of outcome. Again, the practical implications are quite different – and can have significant organisational, cultural and even societal impact.

In both cases, the issue is not that one is right, the other wrong. Rather, it is about recognising that underneath the happy simplicity of headline communications may lie some complex and difficult differences. It is therefore really important to expose and explore the detail and evidence of the situation a coachee is grappling with.

If belonging implies a boundary around a 'space', it also implies that the space contains different rules from other spaces. It can really help coachees to be clear about the:

- Space they are focused on
- The specific boundaries and rules they think apply in that space
- Extent to which those boundaries, rules etc. are explicitly understood and agreed upon.

I have, for example, worked with several experienced coachees confused and irritated by new colleagues who won't do things 'the way we do them here'. People can easily forget that what is habit to them now was once unknown to them too. Unwittingly, they have come to believe that: 'this is how everybody does it, it's just common sense'. As a result, a coachee may express frustration with a newcomer whom they've begun to dismiss as dumb or difficult. The coachee may therefore be shocked to discover that their new staff member's non-conformance may instead reflect the established team's lack of onboarding, transition support or guidance for the newcomer.

From a coaching perspective, the basic point is that belonging can turn out to be a rich and unexpected landscape for a lot of coachees. Clearly, an instinct to belong will cause trouble when a coachee is trying to make a choice about leaving. That's why helping the coachee work out what belonging is really about for them – and how it fits into the life they want – can be useful. It may also provoke a new extended exploration in its own right.

14.4 Making a choice about unhelpful habits

We have looked at a couple of major areas of challenge for coachees. In part, this was to start to see how patterns and other brain tricks can shape and complicate what we do. The examples also help show that it can be complicated and intense work to unpick what is happening and what our coachees want to do about it. Not everything is about the big problems, though.

There are several smaller, more straightforward patterns which can present challenges for many of us. You might be wondering why we should sweat the small stuff, but, as the saying has it:

Coaching with 'I' – some of the practical implications

> *If you think you are too small to make a difference, try sleeping with a mosquito.*

If small things can make a difference, then changing the small bad habits could also have a significant effect on a coachee's working day. The modern world's relationship with technology is a case in point.

The history of our relationship with technology is an interesting one. In recent centuries, big technology (in terms of the processes required to create it, the resulting products and the ways of working involved) has driven/constrained societal and cultural change. Small scale, it drove the development of employment and job roles. Large scale, it dictated where and how people worked and lived. Technology, in all its forms, shaped so many of our work and life habits.

The last 50 years have seen the rise and apparent domination of 'information technology' – the operation of systems of hardware and software to manage the creation and use of information. The latest technology is a curious beast. It has large physical focal points (server bases, component production centres etc.). In one sense, thanks to its networked nature, it is bigger than anything humanity has ever produced. In another sense, we can engage with it through a variety of objects, many of which are highly portable. As a result, devices (and their technology) feel personal, as though they belong to their user. The information technology pitch is that humans are controlling information and their relationship with it. The reality is that information technology (IT) is driving behaviour just like any big technology that preceded it. In particular:

- It is a must-have capability for everyone.
- What sits behind it is so complex that most people are relatively low-skilled users rather than masters of the technology they have.
- People are enabled to do the things the technology allows them to do, but typically in the way the technology allows them to do it.

- IT products are often designed and made by those who specialise in the technology, not in its use in other contexts.
- IT is evolving at a pace faster than humans' collective ability to understand what best to do with it.

I recognise the risk of my sounding like a bit of a Luddite here – that's not my intention. Anyone can readily point to fantastic and enduring benefits from the use of modern technology. But our social and cultural relationship with IT is still immature. The result is often a simmering standoff between IT, organisations and employees or users. Some of this is distorting work-life balance, which in the long run, is likely to have harmful effects.

In fairness, much of what is happening in the work context is IT highlighting and compounding issues that already existed with common business processes. In that sense, IT 'creates opportunities' to identify and address poor practices. The operation of the technology is shaping behaviour too, in seemingly inconsequential ways. However, the cumulative impact on habits, use of time, focus and attention can be a high price to pay for many users. Helping coachees reset the balance of their relationship with some basic business/IT practices can be liberating for them. Let's take a quick look at some of the more common potential flashpoints: meeting, message and device management.

14.4.1 Meeting management

People tend not to be as good as they think they are about preparing for and managing meetings. Yet, organisations seem to end up needing a lot of them. As we saw earlier, a virtual meeting is useful and clearly has a place in the way we work. It is not, however, a simple substitute for face-to-face meetings. Apart from the risks associated with connectivity, screens and data sharing, the cues that enable participants to manage debate and meeting contributions are not the same.

Coaching with 'I' – some of the practical implications

When participants don't know how to manage a meeting, let alone a virtual meeting, the experience can be clunky, waste time and cause irritation for all involved. Moreover, virtual meetings also tend to amplify any bad habits participants may have acquired from face-to-face meetings. Senior staff often see themselves as the victims of this situation and, as a result, they tend to surrender and blame the IT, or expect the IT to come up with a solution.

When people defer to technology as its own authority, they can lose sight of the fact that *they* are running the meetings. Simply establishing and enforcing clear rules for virtual meetings can make a significant difference to their utility, as well as save time and frustration.

14.4.2 Message management

We are talking about variants of email and texts here. Most people have been annoyed by – and guilty of – rushing to the screen in response to the latest ping/smartphone notification tune at work, wherever they are. There seems to be an assumption that because these applications send information quickly, users must move quickly too. The result is that the messaging system invades everyone's lives.

The idea of always being connected can seem very attractive, not least because one of the brain's common framing patterns is about being busy – often equated with being important. Most of the time, however, 'being busy' is simply adding to the body of evidence that gained Pavlov his Nobel prize for training dogs to respond to a bell. If everyone were to make a choice about how to use modern communications, would imitating Pavlov's dogs really be their preferred option?

Gradually, individuals and organisations are beginning to impose limits on messaging: working hours only, shut-down for weekends, managing expectations for response times and so on. This seems like a good start and suggests people are beginning to understand how to rebalance their relationship with technology.

14.4.3 Device management

Many people these days could legitimately add device/app manager to their job profile as one of the more significant tasks they do at work. It is not uncommon to have a work desktop, a work laptop, a personal computer, a work phone, a personal phone, professional social media presence, personal social media presence etc. Note that I include the personal devices/presences because these are increasingly being used as part of employment screening and employee vetting (e.g. checking whether a candidate's Facebook profile and history fits with the employer's preferences). In some instances, employees are also actively encouraged to use their own devices as work devices.

Devices – and the applications that run on them – seem to need constant updating. There may be good reason for that, but many users have drifted into a situation where they spend a significant amount of time managing devices, applications, updates, service contracts etc. Often, users default to doing that 'out of working hours'. If they were to look anew at how they interact with these devices and apps and make a choice about how they want to interact with them, what would that look like?

14.4.4 Helping a coachee take back control of their relationship with IT

In a curious way, humans have sleepwalked into a relationship with IT where it has become a virtual, ever-present, yet dumb manager. I don't think that was the intention and I'm reasonably confident that it's not what most of us want. However, the brain's patterns rejoice in novelty, accessibility, power and connectivity (a sense of belonging), which all combine to make IT desirable. Meanwhile, other patterns (the appeal of being noticed, being valued, being busy) encourage addictive, unhelpful and even unhealthy behaviour. The combination of reward and a need to be busy can become powerful and harmful.

Given what we have discussed, when a coachee finds themselves impeded by these relatively low-level habits, their making a choice to

Coaching with 'I' – some of the practical implications

change still feels significant. Interestingly, where I – and peers – have worked with coachees who made a choice to treat IT as a useful tool to be adapted to their needs, coachees typically found that:

- ☐ Their time spent with IT went down.
- ☐ Their productivity went up.
- ☐ They reported feeling less frustrated.

These findings are from a small pool, so are anecdotal rather than definitive. Even so, I strongly suspect they are worth further investigation, which may in turn help us improve our coachees' ability to spot and address those little bad habits at work.

In the end, habits are just that: established patterns of behaviour, which means, of course that they can be difficult to shift. The CHOICE model is one possible response. Equally, NLP and CBT, among others, offer well-established techniques for breaking old habits and embedding new ones In essence, the key step is for the coachee to identify the conditions when the bad habit occurs, to help them:

- ☐ Acknowledge the moment of risk and stop what they are doing.
- ☐ Consider other options (these may be pre-agreed routines).
- ☐ Pursue a better option.
- ☐ Understand and prime the support they will need (which may be rewards, other people, activities).
- ☐ Keep doing their better option until the new habit settles in.

14.5 Making a choice about balance

Image by: Riccardo Ginevri on unsplash

The balance conversation often crystallises in a discussion about 'work-life' balance. The first step tends to be to work out what's causing the balance to fall out of line. Typical causes include:

- Responding to a blockage/risk/threat. The desire for balance may be a reaction to something going wrong, such as a career stalling, or dealing with a personal break up. Clearly, the negative impact may be destabilising, which may hold a coachee's attention. The remedy, however, may lie more in the coachee's dealing with the blockage rather than trying to compensate for it by re-jigging other parts of their life.

- Wanting to get back in control. When things are overwhelming, trying to rebalance is one way to attempt to reassert control. This may be effective, but helping the coachee clarify in detail what is driving their desire to rebalance may identify a more useful line for the coachee to explore.

- Wanting to rebalance for a different outcome. This is about making a positive intervention in the belief that we will be happier/more content as a result.

Coaching with 'I' – some of the practical implications

14.5.1 The personal investment account

Everyone has a limited number of hours in the week and thus has a choice:

- ☐ They can chase as much as possible and hope that will be good enough. Or,
- ☐ They can treat their time like the valuable commodity it is, which needs to be invested carefully.

Anyone can treat their time like an investment asset and manage their own 'investment account' – and judge the value of their choices by the return on their investment. A coachee may thus make a choice to rebalance in order to maximise return on the investment of their time. Promotion and more money may be their desired return, but time with friends or family may matter more.

Note also that individual priorities change over time. What I cared most about as a 5 or 15 year old is somewhat different from what drove me at 50. This is normal. So, it follows that the balance that makes someone happy will change over time too. Unfortunately, many people find that recognising the need to rebalance often lags behind what's happening; that they tend not to notice until something goes wrong. In practice, they may then fail to deal with the thing that went wrong, or to rebalance in order to get where they want to be. As a tool, a personal investment account can help coachees identify and manage the things that matter most to them.

14.5.2 Using the WHOM Map to help the balancing conversation

I developed the WHOM Map to help coachees explore how they invest in Work, Home, Others and 'Me' (WHOM). The idea is simple enough:

- ☐ Mark up a piece of paper as per the illustration overleaf. Ideally, do this on a sheet of paper at least A3 in size.
- ☐ The map has 4 primary dimensions: Work, Home, Others, Me (WHOM).
- ☐ Agree the time frame that this exercise covers with the coachee. Typically, coachees map out a period of 12-18 months. But if it's a really hectic time, 6 months may make more sense.

- ☐ Invite the coachee to add to their map the events, opportunities or risks they consider important. It is generally helpful for them to do this with post-its first, as it can take several attempts to arrive at the map that properly reflects their thinking.
- ☐ Any items falling within the next three months should be placed within the circle. Items further out in time should go outside the circle.
- ☐ The coachee should place their post-its in the most relevant area. So, the post-it for an audit report for corporate assurance is going to land somewhere in the Work-Others area of the map. If, however, the audit is for personal benefit (e.g. to help a new manager understand the operation they are taking on), then the audit would land somewhere in the Work-Me area.
- ☐ As the process can take some time, I would normally work though one or two examples with the coachee in session, but then invite them to complete the map in their own time.
- ☐ Let the coachee complete their map to their satisfaction. But don't let them take too long – 'by the next session' should be the maximum deadline.
- ☐ In session, explore the:
  - ☐ Contents and the coachee's decision-making process.
  - ☐ Overall balance in the map and whether it suits the coachee's needs.
  - ☐ Need/opportunity for any follow-on action.

The WHOM map does a number of useful things. It helps coachees to start working out what matters. For those dealing with a blockage, for example, their rationale for the map they have created will often start to highlight the source of the problem. This then becomes a good first step towards working out how to deal with it. For those needing to get back in control, simply working through the map can help shift their thinking and approach. Where other factors are in play, discussing the overall balance help focus exploration of what needs to change.

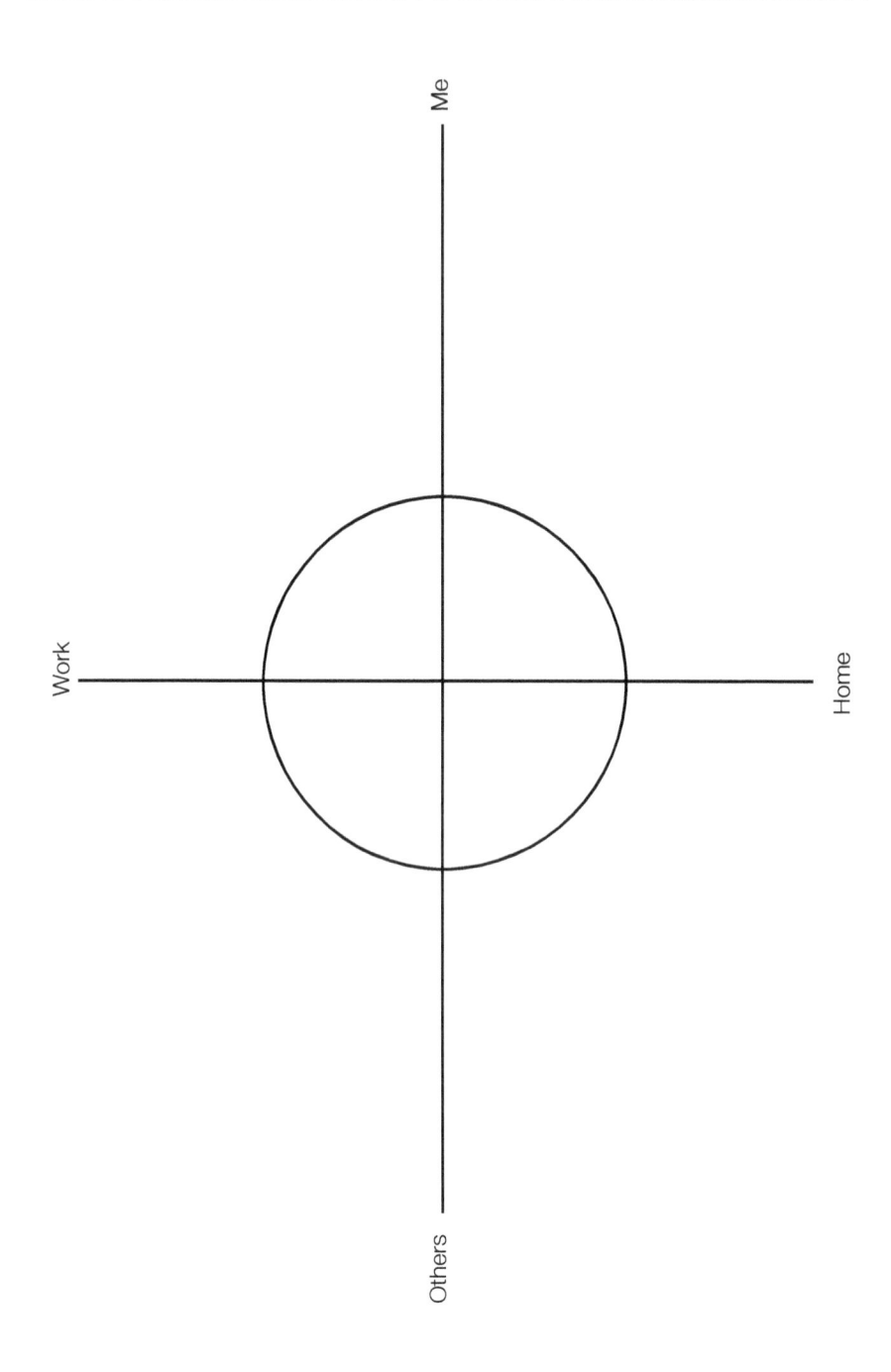

Coaching with 'I' – some of the practical implications

Common challenges

Although this is a simple tool, I should point out that coachees can find it genuinely challenging. If coachees have spent a lot of time caught up in firefighting, they may simply have lost the habit of prioritising. Even without that, what they actually prioritise can be quite different from what they think they prioritise. As a consequence, the process can be a bit sobering for some. But do encourage coachees to persist – they will get a lot out of it.

I should also make the point that, on the question of balance, there is no right answer as such. What matters is whether the balance is suitable for what the coachee is seeking to do at this point in time and for the period covered by the map. The following are summaries of potential map results, which might point to some obvious discussion:

- ☐ A young professional looking for promotion in the next year has a balance that is overwhelmingly in the Work-Others zone. That may raise questions about the pay-off for their investment (promotion), maintaining their health now etc.
- ☐ A Project Manager worrying about burn out has a balance that's overwhelmingly 'within the circle' in all zones. Perhaps they need help to see how to take a step back?
- ☐ A newly qualified professional has a balance that's overwhelmingly in Home-Me. If they're feeling the balance is wrong, then what isn't showing up on their map?
- ☐ Someone 10 years into their career has a balanced map. They and their partner are expecting a baby in the next 3 months. They may be beginning to think – or possibly to avoid thinking – about what happens after the birth.
- ☐ The map is almost blank. Someone overwhelmed or disengaged, perhaps?
- ☐ Every inch of the map is filled in. That might provoke a discussion about delegation, control, self-control.

Coaching with 'I' – some of the practical implications

Working through the WHOM Map helps the coachee define their challenge at a practical, detailed level. That then helps them focus on the choices they want to make about rebalancing.

14.6 Making a choice

We have spent some time looking at four broad areas in life where our coachees might look to make a choice: direction, belonging, unhelpful habits and balance. There may be some common ideas and questions running through all these areas and, as coachees, we are likely to find there are at least some familiar topics for discussion. Nonetheless, the particular combination of themes and personal circumstances of each of our coachees as they grapple with these questions will be unique. The same CHOICE model can be used to help the coachee document and analyse what's going on and how they want to respond.

Making a choice is about identifying those decisions that matter and stopping ourselves from letting automatic/System I/Computer behaviour take – and sometimes mis-take – decisions for us. We may still get things wrong. I hope it's clear, however, that we stand a better chance of getting it right, a better chance of finding a new and more interesting solution – and a better chance of remedying the mistakes we make – if we choose actively to take part in the decisions that matter to us.

Key takeaways

- A small shift in making more choices consciously can have a dramatic impact on outcomes.
- There are several models that can help, CHOICE provides a basic framework anyone can use.
    - **C**onditions. Identify key decisions and the circumstances associated with them.
    - **H**itting pause to invoke our conscious selves
    - **O**utlining the situation – including related emotions.
    - **I**nvestigating our thoughts and feelings. What patterns might be in play? Are they appropriate? What alternate options do we have?
    - **C**hoosing the option that seems most appropriate.
    - **E**nacting our chosen option.
- Making a CHOICE can help with changing: direction, belonging, unhelpful habits and balance.

Conclusion

As I said in the Introduction, this journey started with my trying to understand how beliefs, values and drivers came about and how this might drive our choice/decision making. In particular, I wanted to understand how sometimes these thoughts could be misplaced, yet we still hold onto them, despite compelling contrary evidence. This led me to some fascinating encounters with the worlds of biology, psychology, sociology, neuroscience and even neuroeconomics. Quite properly, those worlds are primarily focused on their own goals and objectives. What was harder to come by was a more holistic view on how these come together to inform our understanding from a coaching perspective of:

- How our brains work.
- The conscious mind and personality that appear to dwell within our brains.
- How brain and mind work to guide our decisions – mostly to our benefit, but sometimes to spectacularly unhelpful effect.
- How our understanding of this process might shape our approach to coaching.

I set about trying to make sense of that narrative for myself and potentially others. Along the way, it became clear just how brilliant and flawed the brain is. It also became clear just how few conscious choices we make. For good reasons, the brain employs a whole range of tricks to save time and energy. Because that activity happens below our consciousness, however, we lose sight of the patterns that quietly determine so much of our lives.

We accept the convenience of automatic behaviour – for the most part, it serves us well. But that does mean that we can too easily find ourselves making the wrong decision for the wrong reasons. Worse, we may start to repeat the same mistake without understanding why. At a practical level, recognising this state of affairs (or rather, state of mind) should encourage us to adopt a habit of healthy doubt. This is not to fret or question ourselves about everything, but should prompt us to recognise our own imperfection(s). As a consequence, we might more often resist succumbing to a convenient pattern. We might become more mindful of some of the more important decisions we need to make. Instead of sleepwalking into an answer, we can choose what we do and how we do it.

To be fair and clear: more conscious thinking and decision-making does not guarantee that our every choice will be a winner. But the more we can draw appropriately on our experience, critical thinking and the external cues available to us, the better prepared we will be for the future we choose. For the majority of us, that shift of mindset will take practice and learning.

As coaches, if we have a good understanding of the factors shaping the brain's approach to choice/decision-making, mindset, then we should be better able to:

- Establish and maintain an effective coaching relationship.
- Be more aware of our own patterns and processes and so reduce the risk that those patterns inadvertently get in the way of our coachee's journey.
- Help our coachees expose and explore unhelpful patterns in their decision-making.
- Help our coachees evolve a stronger choice-making mindset. To that end, coaching for me is an ideal and safe environment for coachees to:
  - Develop a habit of healthy doubt.
  - Build competence in constructive reflection on the questions and issues they wish to address.
- Actively make choices more of the time about the things that matter to them.

Conclusion

The definitive story of the relationship between brain, mind and personality has yet to be written. No doubt at some point it will be achieved. This book is a snapshot of where we seem to be at the moment from the perspective of a practising coach. We are engaged in a long conversation about who we are, how to make our best, most fulfilled selves – and, from a professional perspective, how coaches can best support that process for their coachees. In that spirit, I hope I have nudged you into thinking a bit more about these issues. Better still, I hope I've encouraged you to roll your sleeves up and join the conversation.

Go on, make a choice.

Afterword

How even simple words can open up a world of deeply held values and beliefs

If you have jumped to this page straight from the introduction to demand satisfaction over my indifference to 'choice' v 'decision', then please stop. This book contains material that will help explain my position and the comments below. So I do think it would be better to read it first! However, if you insist…

I don't acknowledge a significant difference in intrinsic meaning between choice and decision. I opted for 'choice' in the title simply because to me it landed better on the ear – once a language student, always a language student, I guess. For all other practical purposes, it didn't matter whether we wanted to make a choice or a decision. I went through a few reviews of the material in this book and tested several parts of it with peers before publishing. One line of discussion came as a bit of a surprise.

My use of 'making a choice' and 'making a decision' sparked some surprisingly intense and extensive debate. In particular, among those who maintain that an important difference exists between the two phrases, their defence was enthusiastic. In practice, however, some of the claimed differences didn't seem to hold that well. For a more independent view, the internet provided some useful setting out of positions. Broadly, the list of distinguishing factors seems to come down to:

- ☐ Multiple options   v   a simple either-or
- ☐ Freedom   v   Constraint
- ☐ Empowering   v   Disempowerment
- ☐ Emotion   v   Analysis
- ☐ Mindset   v   Process
- ☐ Contingent action   v   Final action.

Afterword

Based on the discussions I had, I'm confident a proportion of you will respond with a sense of 'hm, not sure those differences are there' when you think about this list and 'choice' or 'decision'. Equally, a proportion of you will have a clear view of which is a choice, which a decision – and of which is somehow better. You will have noticed that I didn't identify choice or decision in the sets above. That's because the arguments for the differences turned out not to be entirely consistent and, into the detail, things became even hazier, not to say headache causing.

Some of the conversation around empowerment became a bit tortuous for example when choice (but not decision) was held to be an empowering concept. But in the same conversation, choice could be described as something presented to us – in other words, we were in some sense being constrained.

Empowerment featured a lot in my discussions, but with both choice and decision being defended as empowering by different camps. Empowerment is surely about agency, so lies in the subject of the sentence, not in the use of 'choice' or 'decision'. If I am the one making the choice/decision, that's empowering for me. If somebody else is doing the making, that seems less so. In the end, several discussions started to fall back into Humpty Dumpty's scornful: 'When I use a word, it means just what I choose it to mean — neither more nor less' (CS Lewis (1872) *Alice Through the Looking Glass*). So that's clear then.

Meanwhile, forbes.com (qv) had an interesting take on the idea, suggesting that notions of difference stemmed from ideas on freewill and determinism. Suddenly, we're drawn away from whether it's 'choice' or 'decision', or even the options we have, or which will be the last option standing. Now the battleground is actually about our ability to act as we will.

At this point, the staunch support for choice or decision is starting to look like emotional defence of a position linked to beliefs and values. If you've read the bit of this book between the Introduction and here, you've probably begun to wonder whether a pattern is in play. For me, that's absolutely what's happening.

From a coaching perspective, choice/decision looks like a simple option. However, when even a simple option sparks engagement, emotion and energy, that should alert us to the possibility that something interesting is going on behind the scenes – that patterns are being applied and encountering conflict.

Encouraging a coachee to explain their sense of the difference and which they see as the 'better' option could present a handy doorway into exploring and exposing bigger issues. It could open the way to exposing and exploring beliefs, values and patterns at play in the coachee's approach to the discussion point at hand.

If a question of choice/decision is launching patterns relating to freewill, empowerment, or finality (or indeed their opposites), understanding the cause and usefulness of those patterns seems worthwhile. I say that because we can be confident that if patterns are at work here, they are shaping other, bigger thoughts and decisions. I would therefore encourage you and your coachees to take the time to explore whenever apparently innocent nuances provoke them to intense reactions.

Notes

A note about the notes

The following notes are intended to supplement the main text and point those who are interested towards further reading. The bibliography/references are not exhaustive. In part, this is to make the notes accessible and encourage interest – the book is meant to be a conversation starter, not a formal dissertation. Also, the research in this area is dynamic and constantly evolving our understanding of what is happening. So, one of the few things I can guarantee is that more material will have been published since this book went to press. To that extent, this book, like any other on this subject, will be forced to play catch up. My hope is that by providing sufficient starting points, I will sow the seeds of interest for you to explore further on your own.

I How did 'I' get here

1 The grey matters

1.1 Unexpected power

1. *The brain*. Wikipedia is as good a start as any for the basic biological data, with more than enough textbooks out there to delve further if you wish. There are multiple studies out there about the size and complexity of the brain. The figure of 100 billion neurons seems to be a fair order of magnitude statement – studies seem to point to the 'real' figure being 86 billion, plus or minus 8 billion. I appreciate that some people are keen to see exact numbers, but the fact is, they don't really exist in this space. Even if we could count to the last neuron in a brain, we couldn't guarantee that every brain would have the same count – for a whole host of reasons. These order of magnitude numbers make the main point – the numbers

Notes

are big. To see a little more about how researchers are attempting to do the analysis, you could try:

- Herculano-Houzel S and Lent R (2010) Isotropic Fractionometer: A simple method for the quantification of total cell numbers in the brain *Journal of Neuroscience 25(10) pp2518-21*

2. *Dealing with the big numbers.* The numbers here are quite mind-numbing. Just to set them out a little more clearly, the table below summarises the main orders of number talked about in this book. The reference point is the International System of Units (SI).

Prefix	Short form	English word	Full decimal form
Mega	10^6	Million	1,000,000
Giga	10^9	Billion	1,000,000,000
Tera	10^{12}	Trillion	1,000,000,000,000
Peta	10^{15}	Quadrillion	1,000,000,000,000,000
Exa	10^{18}	Quintillion	1,000,000,000,000,000,000
Zetta	10^{21}	Sextillion	1,000,000,000,000,000,000,000

3. *Supercomputer power.* Lots of websites talk about the current most powerful computer. At the time of writing, this reference is as good as any:

- https://www.weforum.org/agenda/2021/01/supercomputer-world-technology-computer-japan-fugaku/

1.2. Thought seems to be an afterthought

4. *The brain as thinking machine.* I accept that brain, mind and thought are related, but I have deliberately avoided the bottomless can of worms labelled: 'What exactly is the relationship between brain, mind, the conscious and personality?' As soon as we step

Notes

away from the relative certainty of the brain's biology, things become complex and elusive. And, like so much of our discussion about the brain, we seem to be some distance off a clear and comprehensive understanding of how exactly it all comes together. I have the luxury in this book of being able to keep the focus on what seem to be key processes and results. If you are up for a challenge, then there is much more to explore here. For a current starting point, you could try:

- ☐ Ball P (2022) *The Book of Minds* Picador.

As for how the brain came to think, the reference is:

- ☐ Barrett LF (2020) *Seven and a Half Lessons About the Brain* Picador.

5. *Our senses.* Word is getting out that there are more than 5 senses, though the idea that there could be as many as 55 or so would probably still come as a surprise to many. To get started, have a look at:

- ☐ Henshaw JM (2012) *A Tour of the Senses* John Hopkins University Press.

6. *Plato's prisoners.* If you can hack the ancient Greek, by all means do. Otherwise, it's hard to beat the Loeb Classical Library:

- ☐ Plato *Republic Books 6-10*
  trans Emlyn-Jones C & Preddy W (2013)
  Harvard University Press

The main point here is about the representational nature of the brain's interpretation. But the section is worth looking at in full. There are some useful tips for anyone working with change, in that the example highlights the need for those undergoing change to acclimatise. There is also the clear warning that once we have seen things differently and try to persuade the remaining prisoners, we are likely to meet resistance.

In the coaching context, Plato's account is a helpful reminder for our coachees that when they begin to change, their relationship with 'other' begins to change too. They may notice some unexpected issues with or challenges – perhaps even open resistance – to what they are trying to achieve. As a result, they might fear that they are making an error in their new thinking/behaviour. Hence, it is important they have the space in sessions to reflect on any feedback evidence they notice, to clarify whether they are seeing the results of error or peer discomfort.

7. *Brain activity.* Here we enter the world of neuroscience. The field is rich and complex, building knowledge through very detailed and focused research. As a result, much of the emerging material is challenging to read for those of us who are not neuroscientists. You can try to ease yourself in with e.g.:

   ☐ Brann A (2015) *Neuroscience for Coaches* Kogan Page

   But if you really want to keep up, then regular journal monitoring will be required.

1.3 Specialisation

8. *Brain specialisation – Brodmann.* As I say in the main text, the picture is evolving fast, but the Brodmann map is a helpful marker for our discussion. Lots of ways to find out more, but Wikipedia is as useful an introduction as any. Start with 'Brodmann area':

   https://en.wikipedia.org/w/index.php?title=Brodmann_area&oldid=1126946074

   then follow the links out. The Wikipedia pages link to further details on the standard 52 designated areas, again each with follow-on references if you're up for the task..

Notes

1.4 The emergence of patterns

9. *Saul's conversion.* Like so many of my generation, I was brought up with a basic knowledge of the Bible. For those not familiar, the Book of Acts in the New Testament tells how Saul, leading the hunt for Jesus' followers was stopped in his tracks on the road to Damascus. With a flash of light, God commands Saul to do his bidding, which he does. Saul becomes the Apostle Paul, key to the development of the early Christian church. The point here is that awe and wonder are as powerful as awe and thunder when it comes to changing our minds.

1.5 Patterning the future

10. *Cognitive Behavioural Therapy* (CBT). CBT is now standard therapy for a range of mental health challenges. The same tools and techniques can also be used in less debilitating circumstances. As a solid introduction for those new to the ideas, try:

    ☐ Westbrook D, Kennerley H and Kirk J (2011) *An Introduction to Cognitive Behavioural Therapy* (2nd Ed) Sage

    At the practical level, many of the techniques are mirrored in the practices of Neuro-Linguistic Programming (NLP). There is a vast amount of literature on NLP, so take your pick.

1.6 And then there's emotion

11. *The role of emotion.* In western tradition in particular, we are accustomed to distinguishing between reason and emotion. The French philosopher Rene Descartes was the poster boy for this sort of 'dualist' thinking, which came to dominate debate for several centuries. Increasingly, however, that distinction seems less than entirely well-founded. Again, there is no end of academic literature/journals to review if the subject engages you. The references here are:

- ☐ On memory storage: LaBar, KS; Phelps, EA (1998). "Arousal-mediated memory consolidation: Role of the medial temporal lobe in humans" *Psychological Science.*9(6): 490–493

- ☐ On the impact of emotion: Seidner, SS (1991). *Negative Affect Arousal Reactions from Mexican and Puerto Rican Respondents* Washington, D.C.: ERIC

You might also find this helpful:

- ☐ Damassio A (1994) *Descartes' Error: Emotion, Reason and the Human Brain*, New York

For the context of this work, the world of neuroeconomics (which has so far brought together neuroscience, psychology and economics in the struggle to understand the brain) also has some interesting insights on the impact of emotion on decision-making. For a deeper dive into all this you could try:

- ☐ Glimscher PW and Fehr E (Eds) (2014 2nd Edition) *Neuroeconomics: Decision Making and the Brain* Academic Press

- ☐ Christiansen B and Lechman E (Eds) (2016) *Neuroeconomics and the Decision-Making Process* IGI Global

1.8 A word about memory

12. Neuroscience and psychology both have a lot to say about memory, though it feels as though we are still some way off properly understanding it. At the moment, perhaps the more intriguing contribution from neuroscience is in appearing to show that memory processes activate more areas of the brain than were initially assumed. Our instinctive response is probably to assume that 'a' memory is akin to a photo in our smart phone – complete, stable and retrievable as a consistent artefact. It is clear that this is simply not the case.

Notes

The revelation at just how malleable memory is can (and perhaps should) be unsettling for most of us. As illustrations of the level of malleability, see:

- ☐ Kahana MJ (2012) *Foundations of Human Memory* Oxford University Press

- ☐ Underwood BJ (1957) Interference and forgetting *Psychological Review* 64, pp 49-60

- ☐ Whitely PL (1927) The dependence of learning and recall upon prior intellectual activities *Journal of Experimental Psychology* 72, pp853-858

The further references are:

- ☐ Markowitsch HJ (2000) Neuroanatomy of Memory in Tulving E and Craik FIM (Eds) (2000) *The Oxford Handbook of Memory* Oxford University Press

- ☐ Nyberg L and Cabeza R (2000) Brain Imaging of Memory in Tulving E and Craik FIM (Eds) (2000) *The Oxford Handbook of Memory* Oxford University Press

If you are up for a deeper dive, then there is much in the rest of *The Oxford Handbook of Memory* to keep your mind occupied and help you identify further avenues to explore.

2 The brain's strange universe

2.1 Time isn't what you will think it was

13. 'An idea in the now'. Grosz S (2013) *The Examined Life: How We Lose and Find Ourselves* Chatto & Windus

2.2 Risk and reward

14. *A question of risk.* Neuroeconomics (see note 11) is generating some interesting insights into all this. There is a sense in which the problem with risk is that if our emotional state is off (either too negative or too positive), then we are more prone to distorted risk taking. The implied imbalance invites us to assume that there must be an optimum point (Goldilocks effect again!) somewhere in between. We might even see an app one day to tell us when we are ready to decide something. But I suspect developing a habit of evidence-checking the important decisions will continue to be the more reliable route.

The question of risk also opens up the idea about risk aversion. Kahneman D and Taversky A (1979) (Prospect theory: An analysis of decision under risk *Econometrica* (47) pp263-291) launched the idea, which has lately been challenged. But, anecdotally, it still seems to have practical value. This may be more to do with level of vested personal equity than fear of loss, but there does seem to be something here. Certainly, in my work in management consultancy I found that risks tended to be discounted when formed as 'x could happen', but provoked rather more discussion when framed as 'if x happens, you will be liable for y' (especially if 'y' was a financial figure or touched on the personal reputation/career of the decision maker). In other words, the perception of risk changes dramatically between a 'risk out there' and a risk to you as an individual.

2.4 Patterns

(this also applies to chapter 3.Some common patterns)

15. The material on patterns draws on a range of sources, including personality assessment models and business, as much as psychological material. The intent here is to focus on the practical impacts rather than to deep dive into some of the debates that exist. In particular, there seems to be a fault line between models

developed in the business world (mainly because they seem to work well enough in practice) and models that have been subjected to academic testing standards. Both sets of models tend to claim to meet rigorous scientific standards.

For the more common tools (which play into tied patterns (see note 21), there is so much material out there, you'll be spoilt for choice. Wikipedia is as good a starting point as any, then follow the leads from there:

- ☐ MBTI:
  https://en.wikipedia.org/w/index.php?title=Myers%E2%80%93Briggs_Type_Indicator&oldid=1131358744

- ☐ Keirsey Temperament Sorter:
  https://en.wikipedia.org/w/index.php?title=Keirsey_Temperament_Sorter&oldid=1104447429

- ☐ DISC:
  https://en.wikipedia.org/w/index.php?title=DISC_assessment&oldid=1120896796

- ☐ Belbin Team Inventory:
  https://en.wikipedia.org/w/index.php?title=Team_Role_Inventories&oldid=1124084591

- ☐ NLP:
  https://en.wikipedia.org/w/index.php?title=Neuro-linguistic_programming&oldid=1130636778

- ☐ Enneagram of Personality:
  https://en.wikipedia.org/w/index.php?title=Enneagram_of_Personality&oldid=1131020938

We need to recognise that some things work because of the placebo effect: 'do this and feel better' guidance does often result in people feeling better for a while at least. Placebo 'wins' may be less rigorous and satisfying than fully documented methodology, but that doesn't mean they can't be useful. The psychological material underpinning pattern references here is endless. There is a range of psychology primers, all of which cover the material. It really is a question of picking one that works for you as a starting read.

3 Some common patterns

3.3. Framing patterns

16. *3.3.4. Confirmation: Blackadder* was a British comedy series that first aired during the 1980s. If you needed this explanation, then I strongly recommend you find a way to watch them all – now. *Line of Duty* is a British Police series that has been running since 2012. The Hastings interview has become something of a set piece for the series.

3.4 Authority patterns

17. *3.4.2 Bandwagon: The longest line.* Asch's experiments on conformity were published in the 1950s:

    - Asch S (1951) Effects of group pressure on the modification and distortion of judgement, in Guetzkow H (Ed) *Groups, Leadership and Men* Carnegie Press

    - Asch S (1956) Studies of independence and conformity: I. A minority of 1 against a unanimous majority *Psychological Monographs: General and Applied 70(9) 1-70* 1956

    Concerns were raised about the methodology, test group size and structure. But this concept does seem to have some merit outside the laboratory.

18. *Groupthink.* Coined by WH White Jnr in 1952 (Fortune, March 1952, p114-117), the concept was given some research oomph by IL Janis in 1972 (*Groupthink: Psychological Studies in Policy Decisions and Fiascoes* Houghton Muffin).

Notes

3.5 Overconfidence patterns

19. The shark cartoon was created on Canva Free.

3.5.1 Distorted valuation

20. *Dunning-Kruger effect.* See:

- ☐ Kruger J & Dunning D (1999) Unskilled and unaware of it: how difficulties in recognising one's own incompetence lead to inflated self-assessments *Journal of personality and social psychology* 77(6) p121.

The title says it all, really.

3.6 Tied patterns

21. *Personality profiling.* This story begins about 2,500 years ago in the world of ancient medicine. Alcmaeon of Croton is said to have developed a medical theory of humours, further developed by Hippocrates. The idea began as a focus on health and what our health state does to our temperament and behaviour. The extension of the thinking to emotion and personality modelling would evolve over another 1,900 years or so. The next big leaps came really with Carl Jung (*Psychological Types*, 1921) and Hans Eysenck (*Dimensions of Personality*, 1947). The second half of the twentieth century saw the growth of personality assessments effectively based on these principles. In the business context, Myers Briggs Type Indicator® (MBTI) and a range of DISC-based models (Dominance, Influence, Steadiness, Compliance/Conscientiousness) are the most common (see note 15). Within 'academic' psychology, the 'Big Five (Openness, Conscientiousness, Extraversion, Agreeableness, Neuroticism) seems to be the best documented and evidenced. But be aware that there is lively debate in that arena too.

Add more detailed research as you progress. Note that, whichever model you like, (variants of) the Type B scales and Type A groupings or elements appear in multiple models. For example, I've used the NLP 'towards/away from' and 'through/in' time headings, but the sub-patterns are clearly visible in the other models (eg The J/P preferences for future v now). See note 15 for basic starting points for your journey.

To gain a better understanding, do a MBTI, DISC or Big Five assessment. However, you will need to become an accredited facilitator if you want access to all the resources.

Sadly, in practice, agendas, vested interests, incorrect use and plain misuse of such tests all combine to put people off. Used properly, the tests can provide a powerful framework for self-assessment and growth.

4 Beliefs, Values and Drivers

4.2 Values

22. There are now lots of takes on the values concept, though they tend to share common features. The two references here are to:

    ☐ Rokeach M (1973) *The Nature of Human Values* New York: Free Press

    ☐ Gouveia VV, Milfont TL, Guerra VM (2013) Functional theory of human values: testing its content and structure hypotheses *Personal Individual Differences* 60 pp41-47

    For me, it seems helpful to think both about the specific value a coachee prioritises and the type of value (instrumental/terminal, personal/social etc.) as both aspects help build a richer map of patterns at play in the coachee's thinking.

23. *Living your values.* See Brown B (2018) *Dare to Lead* Penguin Random House. It is such a simple statement: live your values. Yet it seems to be a common stumbling block. The problems start if we

don't actually know what our values are, then multiply when we realise that (some of) our values are not actually about us or just don't serve us well. To coachees coming new to coaching, talking about values may seem a little up in the clouds. But values so strongly shape our actions that we ignore them or fail to understand them at our peril.

24. *Hierarchy of needs.* As with so much referenced here, there are other options. But Maslow is a useful starting point:

    ☐ Maslow, AH (1954). *Motivation and Personality* New York, NY: Harper & Row Publishers.

    There seems to be a fascination with the fact that he didn't draw his hierarchy as a pyramid. I suggest the more useful conversation would be about the extent to which the lower needs must (continue to) be met for the higher needs to be addressed.

25. *The power of negatives.* See:

    ☐ Covey SR (1989) *The 7 Habits of Highly Effective People* Free Press.

26. *Loss aversion.* See:

    ☐ Kahneman D and Taversky A (1979) Prospect theory: An analysis of decision under risk *Econometrica* (47) pp263-291.

    ☐ McGraw AP, Larsen JT, Kahneman D and Schkade D (2010) Comparing gains and losses *Psychological Science* (21) pp1438-1445

    I am aware in the research community there is ongoing debate about the nature, strength and even validity of these ideas. But, in practice, they continue, successfully, to underpin a lot of thinking about and practice of market analysis and sales activity. On that basis, the concepts remain useful here. It may well be that another factor is causing the behaviour observed. For now, for our purposes, we can recognise that something seems to be driving a stronger reaction to loss rather than gain.

4.3 Drivers

27. *Transactional Analysis* (TA), TA is a well-established theory with a wealth of literature and practical guidance behind it now. For a straightforward introduction, try:

    ☐ Stewart I & Joines V ((2012) *TA Today: A New Introduction to Transactional Analysis* (2nd Ed) Lifespace Publishing

    A lot of coachees seem to find the model relatively easy to begin using.

5 Errors in the machine

28. *A zettaflop.* See note 2 above. I appreciate that some readers will feel a need to place an exact figure on this even as an analogy. We could arguably put a more precise figure to this calculation – but that would be an illusion. The fact is, we cannot assess (at least not for now) the brain in terms of accurate overall computational power or rate of error. The key point is that the basic maths make it clear that our brains must be making lots (that is, in the hundreds of millions' worth of lots) of errors.

5.3 Errors of influence

29. *Nudge techniques.* These have enjoyed a degree of popularity in western governments this millennium in order to improve citizen outcomes. The debate is on, however, about the dividing line between supporting civil improvement and population control. That debate needs to encompass private sector responsibilities too – but that's another discussion. For now, the following may be of interest:

    ☐ CR Sunstein, RH Thaler et al (2009) *Nudge: Improving Decisions about Health, Wealth and Happiness* Penguin (which contains more on the Schiphol experiment)

Notes

- G Del Balzo (2018) *Nudging in the USA, in Denmark, in Italy: an international comparison of Behavioural Insights Teams* Online University Press.

5.4 The truth is out there

30. *My truth.* The point is that *my truth* is a framing pattern. In chapter 3.3 we met the framing patterns of Constraint (applying a limited scope to our thinking) and Discounting (rejecting anything out of scope). When the two frames work in tandem, they can become fierce defenders against any challenge to what the brain thinks it knows. Even the most obvious, irrefutable evidence may be rejected.

    To see just how powerful these patterns can be, consider the experiment of the gorilla in the basketball court. Test subjects were asked to observe part of a basketball game and tasked to count the number of passes made while they watched. During the game, someone dressed in a gorilla suit would briefly appear on the court. Time after time, significant numbers of test subjects failed to see the gorilla. Not surprisingly, many responded to the experimental report and analysis with disbelief – how could anyone miss something so obvious? Well, they did and continue to do so. For a full and more recent account, look at:

    - Chabris C and Simons D (2011) *The Invisible Gorilla* Barnes and Noble.

    The phenomenon they identified was christened: *inattentional blindness*. In the world of subconscious patterns, it is perhaps closer to *intentional* blindess.

    Rashomon, by the way, is a 1950 crime thriller by Akira Kurosawa in which the core theme is the difference between our projected, idealised self and our 'true' self. Now there's a coaching theme.

6 So how did 'I' get here?

6.2 'I' as emergent property

31. Descartes (again) landed with 'cogito ergo sum' ('I think therefore I am': *Discourse on the Method*, 1637). 'itero ergo sum' ('I repeat therefore I am') is offered up to provoke thought. Note that to be able to assert 'I repeat' entails an ability to remember previous thought/action.

32. *Chaos/Mandelbrot*. The first 'popular' introduction to Chaos theory and the associated mathematics (and some more about Mandelbrot) still takes some beating:

    ☐ Gleick J (1987) *Chaos: Making a New Science* Viking Books

    As for apps, a search on <Mandelbrot> or <fractals> will give you enough options to play with!

6.4 A need to be seen

33. *The 'catastrophe of indifference'*. Grosz S (2013) *The Examined Life: How We Lose and Find Ourselves* Chatto & Windus. In a connected, visual universe, it does feel as though we are overdue a full, honest and measured debate about our relationship with 'social' technology.

7 The coaching context

7.1 The inner context

34. *Integrative Relationship Model*. For the original see:

    ☐ Erdös T, de Haan E & Heusinkveld S (2020): Coaching: client factors & contextual dynamics in the change process *Coaching: An International Journal of Theory, Research and Practice*

Notes

35. *Transference and counter-transference.* Freud himself may be out of fashion, but many of the debates he started continue to be relevant today. Transference and counter-transference can pose genuine challenges in therapeutic or coaching/mentoring relationships. They are usually characterised as:

   ☐ *Transference*: an unconscious redirection of feelings from one person (for us, the coachee) to another (the coach)

   ☐ *Counter-transference*: when the therapist (coach in our case) projects their own unresolved conflicts onto the client (coachee).

   For the original references:

   ☐ Freud S: Strachey J (Ed and Trans) (1940/1949) *An Outline of Psychoanalysis,* WW Norton and Company

   ☐ Freud S (1910/1957) The Future Prospects of Psycho-Analytic Therapy

   In Strachey J (Ed and Trans) (1957) *The Standard Edition of the Complete Psychological Works of Sigmund Freud* Vol 11 Hogarth Press.

36. *Parent/Child.* The basic Transactional Analysis model (see note 26 for reference) describes three 'roles': Parent, Child and Adult. Ideally, we should spend most of our adult life operating in Adult space. However, in practice, many of us tend to spend more of our time than we should in Parent or Child!

8 Insights from the world of learning and development

37. *The competence cycle.* See:

   ☐ Broadwell MM (1969) Teaching for learning (XVI) *The Gospel Guardian* 20(41) pp1-3a.

8.1 Learning and learning styles

38. *The learning cycle.* See:

- Kolb DA (1984) *Experiential Learning: Experience as the Source of Learning and Development*, Prentice Hall.

39. *Learning styles.* See:

- Honey P and Mumford A (2006) *The Learning Styles Helper's Guide* Peter Henley.

40. *VAKOG.* As per note 9, pretty much any NLP primer offers more details on the role of these 5 modes for those who wish it.

8.2 Conditions for learning

41. '*It is a truth …*' lands from Jane Austen's 1813 classic *Pride and Prejudice*, wherein she deftly demonstrates that the 'truth' in question is not universally acknowledged at all. Unhappily, too many cultures claim to acknowledge the importance of learning, but fail to act to ensure it. As for the evidence for impact, you can find it wherever you turn and a simple Google search should keep you fully occupied for a rainy afternoon if you want. But for a flavour of some of the thinking, you could try the Borgen Project's Top 10, suggesting that education/learning:

- Is important in the creation of any democratic society
- Is needed to make a society geopolitically stable
- Leads to economic prosperity in the global marketplace
- Gives people the knowledge they need to elect capable leaders
- Helps promote tolerance
- Helps societies change for the better
- Helps societies learn from past mistakes

Notes

- Is a step towards greater equality
- Reduces crime
- Creates hope for the future.

(https://borgenproject.org/effects-education-has-on-society/)

42. *Broadwell* – see note 37.

9 The core coaching intentions: expose, explore, evolve

9.1.4 Articulating our change journey

43. I focused on soft skills because they are so common as a coaching focus; and so critical to performance at senior levels. For basic references, see the Harvard Business Review report completed by:

- Kauffman C & Coutu D (2009). *HBR research report: The realities of executive coaching* available at coachingreport.hbr.org (Accessed 10 August 2020). These findings are backed up subsequent material. For a recent update with a strong coach perspective, try:

- de Haan E (2019) *Critical Moments in Executive Coaching* Routledge.

44. *Personality assessments.* See note 21.

10 Models for talking about the mind

10.1 System I – System II thinking

45. See:

- Kahneman D (2013) *Thinking, Fast and Slow* Farrar, Strauss and Giroux.

10.2 The Chimp paradox

46. For the basics, see:

- Peters PS (2012) *The Chimp Paradox* Vermillion.

To explore current activity and events, head to Chimp Management Ltd's site https://chimpmanagement.com

11 Coaching focus

47. Schools of thought, tools and techniques for supporting coachees come from a range of places. Most of the providers of personality assessment offer materials to work with coachees, within their model. There are established coaching models – though, as I said, for tools and techniques *We Coach* (Passmore et al, 2021, Libri Publishing) takes some beating as a starting point. Similarly, the different schools of thought in psychology have their own way of doing things. From a coaching perspective, I would recommend:

- Palmer S & Whybrow A (Eds) (2019, 2nd Edition) *Handbook of Coaching Psychology* Routledge

for its current survey of relevant ideas being put into practice.

11.2 Coachee focus

48. What coachees want. The HBR report was completed by:

- Kauffman C & Coutu D (2009). *HBR research report: The realities of executive coaching* available at: coachingreport.hbr.org (Accessed 10 August 2020)

These findings are backed up by subsequent material. For a recent update with a strong coaching perspective, try:

- de Haan E (2019) *Critical Moments in Executive Coaching* Routledge.

Notes

49. *11.2.2 Being seen.* To explore the deeper questions around personality, I suggest you start with Wikipedia, then work your way out. In part, you'll circle back around the preference/trait debate – so look at those references. Then, if you're up for it, maybe go round the buoy again with Freud, Jung and the 'Big Five' (see note 20) and dip into:

- ☐ Allport GW and Odbert HS (1936) Trait names: a psycholexical study *Psychological Monologues 47(1)*

- ☐ Eysenck HJ (1970) *The Structure of Human Personality* (3rd Ed) Methuen

for a bit more on trait thinking. Then, just to stir things up, do some searching on personality and 'social learning', 'humanistic' and 'psychodynamic'. That should be more than enough to demonstrate that the matter is far from settled.

Remember that 'validation' is about acknowledging thoughts/feelings, not endorsing nor encouraging them.

12 Contracting for coaching

50. The reference is:

- ☐ Passmore J et al (2021) *We Coach* Libri Publishing

12.1 Stakeholder aims and authority map

51. The references are:

- ☐ de Haan E (2019) *Critical Moments in Executive Coaching* Routledge

- ☐ Kauffman C & Coutu D (2009). *HBR research report: The realities of executive coaching* available at: coachingreport.hbr.org (Accessed 10 August 2020)

- ☐ Passmore J (Ed) (2015) *Leadership Coaching* (2nd Ed) Kogan Page

12.2 Coachability

52. *Growth mindset. See:*

- Dweck CS (2008) *Mindset the New Psychology of Success* Ballantine Books

12.3 Commercial accountabilities

53. *Data protection obligations.* Although data protection concepts (and legislation) have been around a while, I think it is fair to say that the subject is still more discussed than understood. Changes to the general data protection regulations in the UK significantly extended the application of relevant rules. In the UK at least, understanding and compliance are still 'work in progress'. As a consequence, we cannot assume, as coaches, that an organisation we are contracting with understands and is correctly applying current legislation. We do therefore need to be better at understanding and meeting our obligations. For UK coaches, the best place to start is:

- The Information Commissioner's Office: https://ico.org.uk/

12.4.1 Can we not just focus on ROI?

54. It's worth looking at:

- Grant AM (2011) Is it time to RE-GROW the GROW model? Issues relating to teaching coaching session structures *The Coaching Psychologist* 7(2) The British Psychological Society

- International Coaching Federation (2009) *Global Coaching Client Study Executive Summary,* April 2009 at : https://researchportal.coachfederation.org/Document/Pdf/abstract_190

- Kettley P & Strebler M (1997) Changing roles for Senior Managers The Institute for Employment Studies Microgen UK Ltd

Notes

- de Haan E (2019) *Critical Moments in Executive Coaching* Routledge.

12.4.2 Non-ROI coaching benefits for senior/ executive coachees

55. The starting references here are:

- De Meuse KP, Dai G and Lee RJ (2009) Evaluating the effectiveness of coaching: beyond ROI *Coaching: An International Journal of Theory, Research and Practice* 2(2) pp117-34

- Williams S and Offley N (2005) *Research and Reality: Innovation in Coaching* NHS Leadership Centre

- de Haan E (2019) *Critical Moments in Executive Coaching* Routledge

- Kauffman C & Coutu D (2009). *HBR research report: The realities of executive coaching* available at: coachingreport.hbr.org (Accessed 10 August 2020)

- Passmore J (Ed) (2015) *Leadership Coaching* (2nd Ed) Kogan Page

- Strozzi-Heckler R (2014) *The Art of Somatic Coaching* North Atlantic Books

- Albon-Metcalfe J and Mead G (2015) Coaching for transactional and transformational leadership in Passmore J (Ed) (2015) *Leadership Coaching* (2nd Ed) Kogan Page

12.4.5 Capturing the whole impact

56. *Balanced scorecard for monitoring coaching impact.* I quite like the Leedham model, but I leave it to you to consider others/develop your own as you see fit. The reference for the original paper is:

- Leedham M (2005) The Coaching Scorecard: a holistic approach to evaluating the benefits of business coaching

International Journal of Evidence Based Coaching and Mentoring 3(2) pp.30-44.

57. In terms of value for coaches, the further reference is:
    - ☐ Carter A and Peterson DB (2016) Evaluating coaching programmes in Passmore J (Ed) (2016) *Excellence in Coaching The Industry Guide* Kogan Page.

13 Getting the coaching work started

13.4 Using media effectively

58. As I say, the evidence has been consistently in favour of face-to-face over virtual meeting for decades. For a couple of more recent examples, you might try:
    - ☐ Guo Z, D'Ambra J, Turner T, Zhang H, Zhang T (2006) *Effectiveness of meeting outcomes in virtual versus face to face teams – a comparative study in China* presented at the Americas Conference on Information System (ACMIS) 2006
    - ☐ Honovar SG (2021) Physical or Virtual? Or is there a middle path? – Reimagining conferences in the COVID 19 era *Indian Journal of Opthalmology* March 21 69(3) 475-476

COVID made the subject something of a hot topic again; and there are clearly some parties out there with strong views. The material does therefore need to be read with care. Quite a lot of studies are based on self-reporting (i.e. variants of: members of group A think they are more/less productive as a result of having more/fewer physical/virtual meetings). I hope you agree by now that relying on perceptions can be dangerous. Research based more on outcomes (which may be observed behaviour, tangible outputs or other independently measurable data) seems more likely to deliver a useful understanding over time. Many of the studies do, however, point to ways to improve virtual meetings, which seem consistent

Notes

with the points made in chapter 13.4.

For all that, new evidence suggests that, for coaching at least, any gap might not be so significant. It's early days still and collecting reliable data remains tricky. Even so, I recognise that I may need to change my view at some point – steeling myself already. In the meantime, de Haan's critical campaign to bring quantitative rigour to our industry continues. So, check out:

- ☐ de Haan E (2021) *What Works in Executive Coaching* Routledge

14 Making a choice

14.3 Making a choice and belonging

59. *Conformity.* Milgrim ran a series of experiments in the 1960s-70s. Like a number of post-war explorations, this work reflects thinking and debate about the so-called 'Nuremberg Defence' (defendants at the war trials basing their defence on the idea that they were obeying orders). In his experiments, Milgrim claimed to observe full compliance from c.65% of test subjects. The experiments and their reviews sparked considerable debate, both in terms of their relevance to the Nuremberg Defence, but also about the validity of the experiments themselves.

Rather like the Asch experiments (see Note 15), beyond the debate, there does seem to be practical corroboration for low/unquestioning obedience in a range of circumstances. Again, Milgrim's particular explanation may turn out not to be correct. Take a look for yourself at:

- ☐ Milgrim S (1963) Behavioural study of obedience *Journal of Abnormal and Social Psychology* 67(4): 371-8.

- ☐ Milgrim S (1974) *Obedience to Authority:* an Experimental View Harper Collins.

14.4 Making a choice about unhelpful habits

60. *Sleeping with a mosquito.* This is a phrase I've known for a long time, but getting at its origins proved challenging. The Dalai Lama is often credited with the statement. Equally, it is said to be an old African proverb. I have also seen attribution to the Dalai Lama, quoting an African proverb. I even found one account suggesting that the Dalai Lama coined the phrase a long time ago and it has now become an African proverb! For our purposes, I think I'm going to give in. Thank you to whoever first coined the phrase, which contains an important, practical truth for all of us.

61. *14.4.2. Message management.* Pavlov's work on *conditional reflexes* as he called them has been pored over and played with for over a century now. There are lots of different takes on his work and its implications. As a more modern starting point, perhaps lead with:

   ☐ Todes DP (2002) *Pavlov's Physiology Factory* John Hopkins University Press

Index

Albon-Metcalf J. and Mead G. 151, 230
Allport GW. and Odbert HS. 228
Anchoring 45
Approximation 6, 19, 20, 21, 33, 64, 112, 118, 170
Asch S. 44, 217
Austen J. 225
Availability 44, 169

Ball P 213
Bandwagon 44, 64, 217
Barrett LF 4, 210
Baseline 133, 148, 157,
  Profile 159–160
  Tools 160–161
Belief xii, 1,6, 11, 14–15, 17, 20, 23, 27–28, 54–60, 66, 71, 75, 78, 85, 99, 101, 102, 161–168, 180, 183, 185, 195, 202, 205–207, 219
  Enabling 55
  Limiting 56
  Qualifying 55
  Risky 56
'Big 5'/OCEAN 161
Boundaries 40, 107, 109, 137, 179, 187–188
The brain 1, 2–11, 13–20, 22–25, 26–34, 37, 40, 45, 56, 60, 66, 67–68, 70, 72–78, 83, 98, 107, 112, 116–123, 153, 174, 176, 189, 192–193, 202, 208–214
  Computational power 2–4, 208–209
  Errors 62–66, 78
  Stress 16–17, 31, 63, 64, 176, 181
  Suggestion 65
Brann A. 211
Broadwell MM. 94, 102, 224
Brodmann map 7–9, 22, 211
Brown B. 57, 219
Bubblethink 102

Cabeza R. *see* Nyberg L and Cabeza R
Career development 110, 126, 127, 129, 166
Carter A. and Peterson DB. 153, 231
Cause and Effect *see* Patterns Causal Patterns
Chabris C. and Simons D. 222
Change 16, 23, 52–56, 65, 70, 75–79, 83, 91, 93, 95, 99, 108–114, 116–126, 141–145, 148–157, 173–178, 190, 210, 226
Chaos theory 73
  The Chimp Paradox 73, 120–122, 173, 227
Christiansen B. and Lechman E. 213
Client coachability 138, 141–142, 229
  Cultural differences 142–143
  Cultural/ethical fit 142–143
  Trust and rapport 144
Coachee focus 124–128, 227
Coachee self-reporting 152
Coaching ix–x, xiii, 1, 2u7, 34, 36, 54, 57, 66, 70, 79, 81–91, 95, 96, 101, 106–115, 124–130, 135–157, 159–171, 175–178
  Inner context 84–87, 223
  Outer context 88–89
  Using media effectively 169–171
  Coaching metrics 113, 130, 139, 147–156
  Coaching Benefits Pyramid 152–156, 220
Cognitive Behavioural Therapy (CBT) 15, 175, 194, 212
Cognitive cycle 14, 17–19, 22, 24, 30, 54, 63, 64, 84, 116, 174, 177
Commercial accountabilities 82, 89, 137, 144, 148, 229
Competence and development 47–48, 93–102, 110–112, 127, 203, 224

234

Index

Complex dynamic systems 72–73
Confirmation *see* Patterns Framing
(The) Conscious 27, 29–32, 58, 60, 76, 78–79, 116–122, 163, 174, 202, 206
Constraint see Patterns Framing
Contracting 82, 113, 133–156, 228
 See also Commercial accountabilities
Counter-transference 86, 224
Coutu D. *see Kauffman C. and Coutu D.*
Covey S. 58, 220
Cult of the Hero *see* Patterns Authority

Dalai Lama 233
Damassio A. 213
Del Balzo G. 222
De Meuse KP. 150, 230
Descartes R. 212–213, 223
Direction *see Tied Patterns*
DISC 216, 218–219
Distorted valuation 47–48, 218
Drivers xii, 54, 59–60, 71, 75, 78, 85, 161, 166, 168, 202, 219–221
 Scripts 59, 120, 122
Dunning–Kruger 47, 218
Dweck CS. 142, 229

Emotion 9, 15–19, 23, 28, 34, 58, 64, 78, 84, 85, 95–96, 112, 120, 163, 177–178, 207, 212–213, 218
Equality 188
Erdös T. 84–87, 223
Ergonomics 6, 125
Evidence 4, 7, 18, 22, 28, 30, 67, 74, 79, 109, 135, 148, 156, 160, 166, 168, 176, 180, 188, 215, 218, 231–232
 Evidence-based feedback 151–152
 Importance of evidence 112–114
Exclusion *see* othering
Expose, explore and evolve 101–115, 178 183, 226
Eysenck H. 218, 228

Fairness 188
Fehr E. *see Glimscher*

Fight, flight or freeze 16, 100
Freud S. 224

General Data Protection Regulation (GDPR) 152, 162–163
Gleick J. 247
Glimscher PW. and Fehr E. 213
Goldilocks effect 45, 215
Gouveia VV. 57, 219
Grant A. 229
Grosz S. 27, 76, 214, 223
Groupthink 44, 217
Guo Z. et al 231

de Haan E. 139, 148, 149, 152, 223, 226–228, 230, 232
Harvard Business Review see *Kauffman C. and Coutu D.*
Henshaw JM. 210
Herculano-Houzel S. and Lent R. 209
Heuristic(s) 11, 19, 118, 122
Honey P. and Mumford A 97, 103, 224
Honovar SG. 231
'I' 1, 2, 6, 17, 26, 29, 66, 68, 70–75, 79, 113, 116–123, 163–166, 208, 223
 A need to be seen 76–77, 130, 223
 As emergent property 77–79
 As mystical entity 71–72
 Sense of self 2, 26, 163–166
Imposter syndrome 107, 112, 180
Inattentional blindness 222
Indifference machine 76–77
Information Focus *see* Patterns Tied
Information Technology (IT) 190–194
Integrative Relationship Model (IRM) 84–87, 223
Intellectual Property (IPR) 146
International Coaching Federation (ICF) 148, 229
International System of Units (SI) 209

Janis IL 217
Joines V. *see Stewart I. and Joines V.*
Jung C. 161, 218, 228

235

Kahana MJ. 214
Kahneman D. 118, 226
  And Tversky A. 58
  And McGraw AP. et al 220
Kauffman C. and Coutu D. 127, 139, 150, 226, 227, 228, 230
Kettley P. and Strebler M. 139, 149, 229
Kolb DA. 96, 97, 103, 224

LaBar KS. and Phelps EA. 213
Learning 42, 90, 93–105, 108–109, 114, 116–123, 138, 142, 150, 161, 166, 178, 224–225
  Conditions for learning 98–101, 225
Learning cycle 94–96, 225
Learning style 95–96, 103–104, 114, 225
Lechman E. *see Christiansen B*
Leedham M. 151–156, 230
Lent R. *see Herculano–Houzel*
Lewis CS. 206
Loss aversion 28, 58, 220

McGraw AP. *see Kahneman D.*
Making a choice 78–79, 91, 119–122, 133, 138, 147, 173–201, 205, 232–233
  And direction 179–183
  And belonging 183–189, 232
  And habits 189–194, 234
  And balance 195–200
Management of
  Devices 193
  Meetings 191–192
  Messages 192
Mandelbrot Set 73, 223
Markowitsch HJ. 20, 214
Maslow AH. 57-58, 220
  Hierarchy of needs 57–58, 220
Mead G. *see* Albon-Metcalf J. and Mead G.
Memory 9, 10, 12, 14–16, 18, 22–24, 37, 64, 74, 84, 95–96, 163, 177–178, 213–214
  Distortion 23, 112, 214
  Distributed property 22, 214
  Malleability 23, 64–68, 2214
Meta–competence 101–102, 126

Metrics 113, 130, 143, 147–156
Milgrim S. 184, 232
Mumford A. *see Honey P. and Mumford A.*
Myers Briggs Type Indicator (MBTI) 160, 186, 216, 218–219,

Neuroeconomics 202, 213, 215
Neuro-Linguistic Programming (NLP) 15, 98, 175, 186, 194, 212, 216, 219, 225
Non-ROI coaching benefits 148–156, 230–231
Nyberg L. and Cabeza R. 22, 214

Odbert HS. *see Allport GW.*
Offley N. *see* Williams S. and Offley N.
Optimism bias 28
Othering 183
Our personal investment account 196
Outsight 102

Palmer S. and Whybrow A. 227
Passmore J. 134, 139, 150, 227, 228, 230, 231
Patterns xiii, 1, 2, 10–114, 18–19, 24, 30–34, 36–53, 54–61, 64–68, 75, 77–79, 83–84, 98, 112–113, 119–122, 161, 164, 166, 168, 174–176, 185, 189, 192, 202–203, 207, 212–215, 219, 222
  Authority Patterns 43–46, 217
  Causal Patterns 38–40
  Framing Patterns 40–42, 217
  Overconfidence Patterns 547–49, 218
  Storytelling 36–37
  The wrong pattern 32
  Tied Patterns 49–52, 218
  Patterns turned against us 32–34
Pavlov IP. 192, 233
Personality Assessment 49–50, 52, 70–74, 111, 160, 209, 215–216, 218, 227–228
  Completing an assessment 162–166
Peters S. 120, 227
Peterson DB. *see Carter A. and Peterson DB.*
Phelps EA. *see LaBar KS. and Phelps EA.*

Index

Placebo Effect *see Patterns Causal*
Plato 5, 210–211
Psychology 7, 63, 74, 116, 202, 213, 217, 218, 227

Rashomon effect 67, 151, 222
Return on Investment (ROI) 139, 147–150, 152, 153–154, 229
Reward 12, 24, 28–29, 60, 77, 124, 193, 215
Risk 7, 13, 21, 28–29, 39, 44, 46, 50–51, 56, 58, 66, 68, 89, 94, 107, 137, 142, 145, 151, 152, 165, 169, 171, 176, 179, 181, 185, 194, 195, 197, 203, 215
Rokeach M. 54, 57, 219

Schiphol airport 65
Scope *see Patterns Tied*
SDI 160
Seidner SS. 213
Self-sabotage 185
Sense of self *see* 'I'
The senses 4–5, 34, 65, 170, 210
Simons D. *see* Chabris C.
Single Perspective *see Patterns Framing*
Social media 76–77, 135, 193
Soft skills 48, 110–111, 128–129, 148–149, 165, 226
Specialisation 1, 6–10, 63, 125, 211
Stakeholder 96, 109, 111, 136–138, 144, 146, 147–157, 228
 Authority 139–141
Stewart I. and Joines V. 59, 221
Strebler M. *see* Kettley P. and Strebler M.
Strozzi-Heckler R. 151, 230
The Subconscious 29–32, 58, 62, 79, 116–122, 163, 165, 222

Sunstein CR., Thaler RH. et al 221
Survivorship *see Patterns Causal*
System I, System II Thinking 118–120, 173, 226

Thaler RH *see Sunstein CR*
Thomas PPA 160, 163
Time (and the brain) 5, 13, 19, 21, 23, 26–28, 51, 73, 77, 93, 95, 179, 183, 202, 214–215
Time *see Patterns Tied*
Todes DP. 233
Transactional Analysis (TA) 59, 86, 161, 163, 186, 221, 224
Transferability *see Patterns Overconfidence*
Transference 86, 224
Truth 18, 29, 66–68, 222
Tversky A. *see Kahneman D.*

Underwood BJ. 214

Values xii, 54, 57–58, 59, 60, 65, 71, 75, 78, 85, 114, 160–161, 166, 168, 182–183, 202, 206–207, 219–220
 Instrumental/Terminal 54, 57–58, 219
 Personal, central and social 57, 219

Westbrook D. 15, 212
White W. 217
Whitely PL. 214
WHOM Map 196–199
Williams S. and Offley N. 150, 230
Wisdom of crowds 46.